PRAISE FOR
DEPRESSION AND
ITS TREATMENT

"A CRISP, NO-NONSENSE BOOK that provides . . . generous amounts of straight-forward information on depression symptoms and treatment."
— *Contemporary Psychiatry*

"CONCISE AND COMPLETE . . . indeed a welcome addition to all those in the field of mental health."
— *Books Unlimited*

"ILLUMINATING, factual discussions . . . and question-and-answer sections."
— *Booklist*

"CLEAR AND ENLIGHTENING."
— *Library Journal*

"A WONDERFUL, BRIEF VIEW of what can be done to help a person overcome it or at least identify some of the sources."
— *Essex Journal*

The American Psychiatric Press, Inc., an independent corporation affiliated with the American Psychiatric Association, publishes psychiatric literature for professionals.

Note: The authors have worked to ensure that all information in this book concerning drug dosages, schedules, and routes of administration is accurate at the time of publication and consistent with standards set by the U.S. Food and Drug Administration and the general medical community. As medical research and practice advance, however, therapeutic standards may change. For this reason, and because human and mechanical errors sometimes occur, we recommend that readers follow the advice of a physician directly involved in their care or the care of a member of their family.

DEPRESSION
AND ITS
TREATMENT

NEW, REVISED EDITION

JOHN H. GREIST, M.D., &
JAMES W. JEFFERSON, M.D.

WARNER BOOKS

A Time Warner Company

WARNER BOOKS EDITION

Cover design by Don Puckey

This Warner Books Edition is published by arrangement with American
Psychiatric Press, Inc., Washington, D.C.

Warner Books, Inc.
1271 Avenue of the Americas
New York, NY 10020

W A Time Warner Company

Printed in the United States of America

First Warner Books Printing: April, 1994

10 9 8 7 6 5 4 3 2 1

Contents

Acknowledgments — *vii*

Introduction — *ix*

Other Books By The Authors — *xi*

What Is Depression? — *1*

Questions About Depression — *17*

Am I Depressed? — *27*

What About Suicide? — *39*

How Is Depression Treated? — *43*

Psychotherapy — *45*

Antidepressant Medications — *53*

Electroconvulsive Therapy (ECT) — *77*

Contents

New and Less Frequently Used Treatments   81

Some Common Questions About the Treatment
  of Depression   85

Suggested Readings   103

Summing Up   107

Appendix   111

Index   155

Acknowledgments

This book is the result of contributions from many doctors and patients. We can acknowledge the doctors by name and take pleasure in doing so:

From the Department of Psychiatry at the University of Wisconsin: Richard Anderson, Nancy Barklage, Ronald Diamond, Robert Factor, Carl Getto, John Marshall, William McKinney, and Stephen Weiler.

From elsewhere: John Howard Greist and Thomas Greist of Indianapolis, Robert M. A. Hirschfeld of Washington, DC, Gerald L. Klerman of New York, and Joseph Tally of Grover, North Carolina.

Our patients carefully read and criticized drafts of the book. They suggested many of the subjects addressed and the questions asked and answered. We appreciate their important perspective as much as we admire their courage and resilience in facing depression. Letters from readers of the earlier edition are also reflected in this edition.

Georgia Greist and Bill Marten sharpened their editors' pencils to clarify our cryptic exposition and expunge our medical metaphors and jargon. It is obvious they did not work on the previous sentence.

Jean Clatworthy prepared numerous drafts of the book. Her attention to detail, efficiency, and good humor in the face of deadlines are constant qualities that enhance our effectiveness.

American Psychiatric Press has become a major publishing house for psychiatric titles over the past decade. We admire the professionalism of the staff and appreciate the simultaneous care and speed with which they work.

Introduction

This book is for
  People being treated for depression
  People considering treatment for depression
  People wondering whether they are depressed
  Families and friends of depressed people
  Those who treat depressed patients
  And anyone else interested in depression

It is a guide to understanding
  Depression
  What depression is not
  How depression is treated
  Treatment side effects and how they are managed

We wrote it because we know

Doctors* sometimes forget to ask patients about important information

Doctors sometimes forget to advise patients about important facts

Patients sometimes forget important information

Patients sometimes misunderstand important instructions

We hope it will

Maximize the recognition and proper treatment of depression

Minimize treatment difficulties

Promote the best results for patients

John H. Greist
James W. Jefferson
Madison, Wisconsin
March 1992

*We often use the word "doctor" to indicate psychiatrists and other medical doctors (M.D.s) and osteopaths (D.O.s), as well as psychologists who have doctor of philosophy degrees (Ph.D.s). M.D.s and D.O.s can prescribe antidepressant medications as well as provide all other treatments for depression, including electroconvulsive therapy and psychotherapy, whereas psychologists use only psychotherapy.

Other Books By The Authors

Dr. Greist and Dr. Jefferson are coauthors of *Antidepressant Treatment: The Essentials,* published in 1979 (Williams & Wilkins). Dr. Greist is author of *Obsessive Compulsive Disorder: A Guide* (1989) and coauthor with Dr. Jefferson of patient guides on *Carbamazepine and Manic Depression* (1987), *Valproate and Manic Depression* (1991), and *Panic Disorder and Agoraphobia* (1992).

Dr. Jefferson is director of the Center for Affective Disorders and coauthor of *Lithium and Manic Depression: A Guide* (with John Bohn). He and Dr. Greist have coauthored three professional books on lithium, *Primer of Lithium Therapy* (Williams & Wilkins, 1977) and *Lithium Encyclopedia for Clinical Practice* with Deborah Ackerman (1983), and a Second Edition of the latter book with Deborah Ackerman and Judith Carroll (American Psychiatric Press, 1987). Drs.

Greist and Jefferson also edited *Treatment of Mental Disorders* with Robert L. Spitzer (Oxford University Press, 1982). Their book *Anxiety and Its Treatment: Help Is Available* (with Isaac Marks) was published in 1986 (American Psychiatric Press).

What Is Depression?

Depression means different things to different people. Depression can be a *symptom* (as when a person says, "I feel depressed"), a *sign* (when someone observes, "he looks depressed"), or a diagnosable disorder. When we diagnose *depression*, we mean a disorder of sufficient length, with specific symptoms and signs, that substantially interferes with a person's functioning or that causes great personal distress or both.

It is important to separate depressive disorders from everyday "blues" or sadness, which are not depression. Normal grief accompanying the death of a loved one is not depression either. People with the blues or normal grief may experience short-lived symptoms of depression but usually continue to function almost normally and soon recover without treatment.

From here on, when we use the term *depression*, we mean the *disorders of depression* that need treatment.

Depression requiring treatment affects:

- mood or "spirits"
- thinking (cognition)
- bodily functions
- behaviors

Mood in depression is almost always experienced as sad, blue, "down in the dumps," worried, or depressed. Even if mood does not appear depressed, a person may lose interest or pleasure in most activities. Sometimes mood lifts temporarily when a depressed person receives good news (this is known as a mood reactive depression). Sometimes it does not. At times doctors use the word *affect* instead of *mood*, and they mean essentially the same thing when referring to depression. Depressions are classified as mood or affective disorders.

Depressed *thinking* often takes the form of *negative thoughts* about oneself, the present, and the future. Depressive ruminations are recurrent pessimistic thoughts. Depressed people also frequently complain of poor concentration, poor memory, and difficulty making decisions. *Anxiety*, a sense that something unspecified but dreadful may happen, is often present. Exaggerated fear about specific situations may also occur. As depression becomes more severe, patients may feel helpless and worthless and think their situation is hopeless. Thoughts of suicide are common. In the most severe depressions, delusions (false beliefs that are rigidly held even in the face of strong evidence to the contrary) may appear, sometimes involving themes of crimes the person never committed, serious physical illness that is not present, or poverty when the person is not poor. Occasionally, hallucinations (sensations for which there is no external cause) may occur. These are usually experienced as hallucinations that are heard (usually voices making derogatory comments, but sometimes music, clicks, or other noises) or seen (images of people or flashes of light) and occasionally by hallucinatory experiences of taste, touch, or smell. These most severe depressions are sometimes referred to as "psychotic" depressions. Hallucinations, delusions, and poor judgment indicate that the person has "lost contact with reality."

Bodily or *"vegetative"* functions are often affected by depression. Patients commonly experience appetite disturbance (either decreased appetite with weight loss or, less frequently, increased appetite with weight gain); sleep disturbance (usually insomnia with difficulty falling asleep, staying asleep, and/or early morning awakening with inability to fall asleep again, but sometimes hypersomnia or increased sleep); fatigue (see page 22); decreased energy; lessening of interest in usual activities, including sex; and gastrointestinal symptoms such as dry mouth, nausea, constipation, or, less commonly, diarrhea. Pains sometimes mysteriously appear and may migrate from one site to another and disappear when depression lifts (see page 53).

Behavior changes associated with changes in mood, thinking, and bodily function may vary from minor and largely unrecognized to profound problems with obvious tearfulness, sad expression, stooped posture, and slowed-down (a "retarded" depression) or agitated movements with pacing, restlessness, wringing of hands, and so on (an "agitated" depression). Some people are able to work normally but feel horribly depressed; others are unable to perform daily activities like dressing, eating, washing, or working because of depression. At times, depressed patients may put on a smile in an attempt to cover their depression—the so-called "smiling depression." The most extreme example of depressed behavior is suicide.

Physicians and laymen from antiquity to the present have recognized depression and described it clearly.

In ancient Greece, Hippocrates told of a woman "of a melancholic turn of mind, from some accidental cause of sorrow [who] while still going about became affected with loss of sleep, aversion to food and had thirst and nausea."

Robert Burton's *Anatomy of Melancholy* was published in 1621 and remains a lucid description of depression, showing as well how depression has been a part of humankind's experience through the years: "If there be a hell upon earth, it is to be found in a melancholy man's heart."

"Melancholy," an ancient term, continues to be used to describe very severe depression with loss of pleasure in enjoyable activities, failure to feel better when something good happens, depression regularly worse in the morning, early morning awakening, slowed or agitated physical activity, loss of appetite or weight loss, and excessive or inappropriate guilt.

Shakespeare makes Hamlet's depression clear:

Oh, that this too too solid flesh would melt,
Thaw, and resolve itself into a dew!
Or that the Everlasting had not fixed
His canon 'gainst self-slaughter! Oh, God! God!
How weary, stale, flat, and unprofitable
Seem to me all the uses of this world!
Fie on 't, O fie! Tis an unweeded garden,
That grows to seed,
Things rank and gross in nature
Possess it merely.   (*Hamlet*, I, ii)

Alexander Haig, a physician writing in 1900, caught the essence of severe depression: "In this condition self-reliance is absolutely gone, extreme modesty is common or even habitual, a feather weight will crush one to the dust, and even the greatest good fortune will fail to cheer."

Whether unknown or famous, patients describe depression with similar poignance. (The quote from a patient reprinted here and the one from Joshua Logan are reproduced with permission of William Morrow and Company, publisher of *Moodswing*):

Prior to this I had been overly happy, elated because of having given birth to lovely twins two months earlier. At first I tried to keep my mind occupied by keeping busy around the house, cleaning, and taking care of the babies. However, I soon had no enthusiasm for anything. I seemed to get no pleasure out of living. I had no feeling toward the babies or my other two children. I tried to do extra things for the children because I felt extremely guilty about my lack of feeling. I would do everything in the house quickly and then would find myself with nothing to do. I had no interest in any outside activity or any project that would be of great interest to me in a normal frame of mind. I couldn't concentrate. My mind seemed to be obsessed with black thoughts. My husband took me out frequently to take my mind off things, but even that was an effort for me.

As time passed, these feelings of despair and uselessness increased. I lost ten pounds and had no appetite. I would try to sleep away time but found myself unable to. I had terrible dreams and would wake up often throughout the night with a feeling of panic in the pit of my stomach. This feeling of anxiety was always present, and for no good reason it continued to get worse. I found myself not wanting to go back home when I went out to try to shop, yet I couldn't be alone. No matter what I did, I couldn't concentrate except on questions such as, "What is the matter with me? Am I going insane? What have I done to deserve this? What sort of punishment is this?" I felt that my appearance had severely changed. I felt old and unattractive. I had no sexual desire and became more and more guilty about my lack of sexual interest in my husband. I wondered if I was going through the menopause. Could the change of life make me feel such tension and anxiety?

Eventually I found myself going to sleep earlier at night and wanting to sleep as much as possible. This was the only way my mind would stop thinking the same anxious thoughts over and over again. Shortly after this I began to feel physically ill, my appetite got worse, and my smoking increased. My stomach began to trouble me, and I developed severe daily headaches. One day on awakening I found myself unable to get out of bed. Because I felt physically sick and unable to care for my family I began to think that I had a virus and asked my husband to call the family doctor. He gave me a thorough physical exam with blood tests and urinalysis, and found nothing wrong, but I persuaded him to treat me for a virus anyway. He didn't mention that this might be a masked or hidden depression, with anxiety and physical pain my only complaints.

Several days later, after taking medication, I felt

no better, and I awoke the next morning and felt that I didn't want to live. Nothing in life seemed important or worthwhile, and I thought of ways to commit suicide. These thoughts racked my entire body with fear. I knew then that I was not physically sick and that I had to reach out for another kind of help. I told this to my husband and saw my physician again. Upon hearing what I had to say, this time he prescribed an antidepressant and a tranquilizer. He didn't seem to know too much about what depression was or what kind of medication was needed. He recommended that I see a psychiatrist, which, of course, I couldn't possibly do. After taking the medications for one day I felt even worse. If I had to see a psychiatrist, it meant that I was probably going insane, and this thought made me even more frightened. It was more than I could stand. The fear of being mentally ill was so horrible that I decided to take my entire bottle of sleeping pills rather than face the shame of being a mental patient.

Joshua Logan has helped many people recognize that depression (in his case, manic-depression) is compatible both with great suffering as well as great productivity after recovery:

My first impression was that something had sneaked up on me. I had no idea I was depressed, that is, mentally. I knew I felt bad, I knew I felt low. I knew I had no faith in the work I was doing or the people I was working with, but I didn't imagine I was sick. It was a great burden to get up in the morning and I couldn't wait to go to bed at night, even though I started not sleeping well. But I had no idea I had a treatable depression. I had no idea it was anything like a medical illness. I thought I was well but feeling low because of a hidden personal discouragement of some sort—something I couldn't quite put my finger on. If anyone had told me that I could walk into a hospital and be treated by doctors and nurses and various drugs and be cured I would have walked in gladly and said, "Take me," but I didn't know such cures existed. I just forced myself to live through a dreary, hopeless existence that lasted for months on end before it switched out of the dark-blue mood and into a brighter color. But even then I didn't know I had been ill.

It seemed to me that all friends of the average human being in depression only knew one cure-all, and that was a slap on the back and "buck up." It's just about the most futile thing that could happen to you when you're depressed. My friends never even hinted to me that I was really ill. They simply thought that I was low and was being particularly stubborn and difficult about things. If anyone had taken charge and had insisted that I go to a mental hospital, I probably would have gone straight off. Instead they simply said, "Please don't act that way. Please don't look at your life so pessimistically; it's not so bad as you think. You'll always get back to it. Just buck up."

Abraham Lincoln also knew depression well:

I am now the most miserable man living. If what I feel were equally distributed to the whole human family, there would not be one cheerful face on earth. Whether I shall ever be better, I cannot tell; I awfully forebode I shall not. To remain as I am is impossible. I must die or be better, it appears to me.

More recently, the author William Styron *(Darkness Visible: A Memoir of Madness)* graphically described his own depression:

> What I had begun to discover is that, mysteriously and in ways that are totally remote from normal experience, the gray drizzle of horror induced by depression takes on the quality of physical pain. But it is not an immediately identifiable pain, like that of a broken limb. It may be more accurate to say that despair, owing to some evil trick played upon the sick brain by the inhabiting psyche, comes to resemble the diabolical discomfort of being imprisoned in a fiercely overheated room. And because no breeze stirs this cauldron, because there is no escape from this smothering confinement, it is entirely natural that the victim begins to think ceaselessly of oblivion.

What Causes Depression?

Depression is almost always caused by a combination of factors. Inheritance or genetic predisposition, developmental factors such as early loss of a parent, psychological factors such as intense grief reactions, and stress such as coping with unemployment or physical illness combine to produce a final common pathway to the disorder of depression. Each individual has a pattern of genetic, developmental, environmental, social, personality, and physiological factors that combine to permit or protect against depression at any point in time. Understanding and modifying the contributions of these factors is the goal of clinicians who treat depression.

It is now clear that *genetic factors* are important in many cases of depression. If one identical twin has depression, there is a 70% chance that the other twin will also develop depression at some time. Children, parents, and brothers and sisters (including nonidentical twins) of a depressed person have only a 15% chance of developing depression. More distant relatives (grandparents, uncles, aunts) have about a 7% risk. The risk for people without close relatives who have had depression is about 2%–3%. Decreasing risk of depression with decreasing genetic similarity supports the idea of inheritance of depression.

Another line of genetic research points to the same conclusion. When children whose parents have a history of depression are adopted at birth into families with no history of depression, they are three times more likely to develop depression than natural children of the adopting family.

People who experience *early losses* of important persons may develop some predisposition to later development of depression. Thus, children who lose parents at an early age and do not find a suitable replacement may be more prone to develop depression in later life.

Humans are social animals and if *relationships* are difficult and loneliness extreme, depression sometimes develops. Conflicts with family members, employers, co-workers, employees, friends, and even acquaintances can all take their toll. Death is clearly a major social stressor although at times, as when someone is painfully and terminally ill, it can also be a relief. Grief does not usually develop into depression.

Religious preoccupations and worries about the meaning of life may contribute to or aggravate depression. Religion may also be a source of support and comfort and provide meaning for life that might not otherwise be present during a depression.

Many *environmental stressors* such as financial problems, new jobs, legal problems, retirement, or other changes may contribute to the development of depression.

Medical illnesses such as influenza, mononucleosis, hepatitis, and too much or too little thyroid hormone as well as several medications (including various blood pressure lowering medications, birth control pills, and steroids such as cortisone) and, significantly, alcohol and other substances of abuse may cause or contribute to depression.

It is important to recognize that these risk factors are not guaranteed to cause depression. Some people who become depressed have experienced many of these risk factors. Others have experienced none that can be identified even after careful evaluation. Many people who have one or more risk factors for depression *never get depressed*. Much remains to be learned about the causes of depression.

Depression can also *cause* impaired relationships, job problems, financial stress—many of the things that some people feel bring on depression. But even when the causes are unclear, treatment can help most depressed people. The disruptive effects of depression can be severe and it is important that depressed persons not be blamed for a medical disorder they cannot control.

What Are the Chances
of Developing Depression?

Several studies done in different American communities have found that about 5% of the population can be diagnosed as having major depression at any one point in time (see pages 32–36 for a description of major depression). At least 10% of the population will experience a major depression during their lifetime (some studies find rates up to 25%). Women are at least one and a half times more likely to become depressed than men. Studies in many countries and cultures and across all social classes show similar frequencies of depression. People with a history of serious depression have, on the average, about five episodes during their lifetimes, although the number of episodes varies greatly; some people will have only one whereas others will have many more. Early treatment can decrease the length and severity of depression for most people.

At least 10% of people with depression will also have manic episodes. They are said to have "manic-depressive" or "bipolar" disorder. During mania, mood changes from its normal level to an elevated, expansive, elated, or even euphoric state that patients often describe as being "on top of the world." During a manic episode a person may sleep very little, talk continually and very rapidly, take little time to eat, and experience racing thoughts. At times mania is characterized by irritability, impatience, and discomfort rather than elation and euphoria and often manic and depressive symptoms are mixed together (mixed or dysphoric mania). Sometimes the manic state progresses to a point where judgment is impaired and contact with reality is lost. It may be difficult to understand what a person is saying. Sometimes poorly thought-out decisions are acted on impulsively, with serious financial, social, or occupational consequences for self, family, and others. Hospitalization may be necessary. See page 73 for a discussion of lithium and its role in the treatment of manic-depressive disorder.

The Depressive Spectrum

Some people find it helpful to think of the different kinds of depression as occurring on a spectrum—from mild blues or sadness at one extreme to severe, life-threatening depression at the other. This perspective is shown in Figure 1. Although people sometimes say they are depressed when they are actually feeling blue, sad, or even normal grief, these *symptoms* are *not the disorder of depression* as we define it, and these people usually require no treatment. As people move to the right across the depressive spectrum, they enter the area where the disorder of depression and the need for treatment begin. The further to the right a person moves along the depressive spectrum, the more severely depressed that person is.

Many doctors use the depressive spectrum as a way of explaining the difference between just feeling bad and the disorder of depression. This approach organizes useful information about duration of depression, effect on functioning, symptoms, possible causative factors, and treatment choices.

Summary

Depression is widespread and common. Serious depression affects 5% of the population at any one time, and at least

Figure 1. The depressive spectrum*

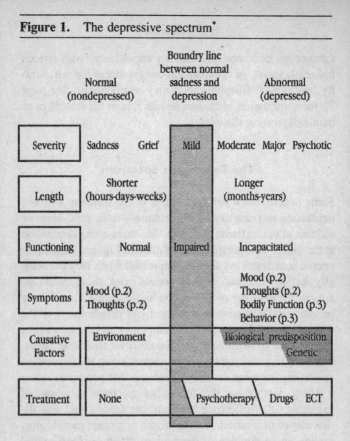

Figure 1 represents a way to symbolize depression. It inevitably oversimplifies the complex phenomenon of depression. Thus there are individuals who have a comparatively mild depression (see the severity category above) that lasts for years (length category) and probably have a genetic predisposition to develop depression (causative factors). Other patients will have very severe but short depressions. Depression is simply not fully understood at this time.

*Adapted with permission from Goodwin FR: "Psychopharmacology in the practice of medicine," in *Diagnosis of Affective Disorders*. Edited by Jarvik ME. New York, Appleton-Century-Crofts, 1977, p. 222.

10% of the population at some point in their lifetime. At least 10% of people with major depression end their lives by suicide.

Although depression spares no segment of the world's population, treatment can restore many sufferers to lives of sensitivity, creativity, and accomplishment.

Many factors are thought to contribute to the development of depression. Depression probably appears when several factors combine in particular ways that are not yet well understood. The occurrence of many different combinations partly explains the many different forms of depression.

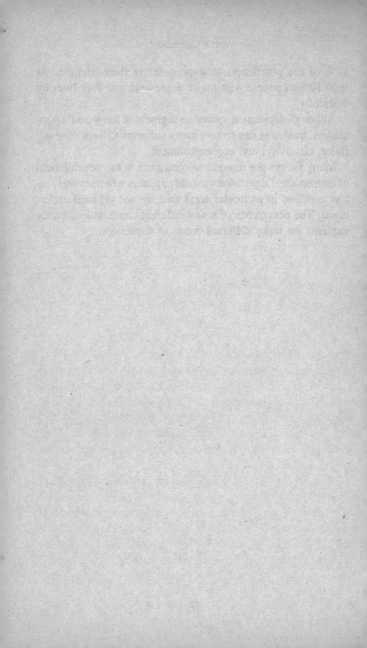

Questions About Depression

Is depression caused by a chemical imbalance? All of our feelings and thoughts, both pleasant and distressing, are the result of electrochemical reactions that occur throughout our brains and bodies. Our present understanding of these reactions and their many interactions is incomplete. It is as though we are in the 15th century and setting out to discover what continents and peoples exist and how they are related to one another.

We have learned, however, from past experience and studies of psychopharmacology (treatment of psychiatric disorders with drugs), that most depressions can be treated with chemicals called antidepressant medications. We do not fully understand the mechanisms of action of these drugs, but together with electroconvulsive therapy (ECT), they are the most effective treatments for severe depression. Although how they work is not fully known, it seems fair to conclude that antidepressant medications and ECT work by correcting "chemical imbalances." Brain chemicals thought to play a role in depression and its treatment include neurotransmitters such as serotonin and norepinephrine. Even if chemical imbalance ultimately proves to explain depression, psychotherapy remains an important component in the treatment of depression. Theories about the cause(s) of depression, whether biochemical or psychological, often tell us little about useful treatment.

Is depression caused by something bad happening in a person's life?   Sometimes it is possible to identify a specific event that appears to have triggered a depression. Even then, the severity of the depression may be out of proportion to the event that brought it on. Often, depression comes on for no apparent reason. This can happen to people whose lives are going well or to people who are having trouble in some area of their lives. It may be that people with a genetic vulnerability are more susceptible to depression set off by bad things that happen in their lives.

Is depression inherited?   It now appears clear that some people have an inherited predisposition to develop some forms of depression. This issue is covered in greater detail on page 9.

How common is depression?   Depression is very common—one of the most common of all mental disorders. At any one time, about 5% of the population is suffering from a major depression. Throughout our lifetimes, at least 10% of us will experience a major depression. Depression is 10 times more common than schizophrenia (a condition characterized by disorders of thinking such as hallucinations and delusions, and by alterations in speech and behavior, some of which may be bizarre) and somewhat more common than the major anxiety disorders (phobia, obsessive-compulsive disorder, and panic disorder).

Community surveys suggest that less than half of the people suffering from major depression are treated. Failure to receive treatment can result in substantial losses of time from work and pleasure in life and family, and even death by suicide.

Do children get depressed?   Children certainly get depressed, although they may not show depression in the same way adults do. For example, sad mood in children may not be described in words but can be seen in persistent sad expressions. Instead of the weight loss seen in adults, children may fail to gain weight as expected. Rather than loss of interest in usual activities or decrease in sexual drive noticed by adults, children may simply show signs of apathy or not caring. Other signs of childhood depression may include acting out or other behavioral problems, and eating disorders that lead to great weight loss or gain. In older children and adolescents, the symptoms of depression may appear very much the same as in adults.

Families often notice changes in children as they become depressed. School work may fall off and previously boisterous and energetic children may become quiet and fatigued. When depression is suspected, the child should be evaluated by a doctor experienced in working with children and depression. Depression in children can be as severe as in adults (adolescent suicide has increased sharply). Children require and respond to the same treatments used with adults.

What about postpartum depression? Following the birth of a baby, the risk of depression is increased in the mother. Possible causes include psychological and social stressors, hormonal changes, and genetic factors. The most common type of depression is a mild form often referred to as the "blues" that occurs in up to 50% of women. It begins within days of delivery up to several weeks later, is of relatively brief duration and severity, and responds well to reassurance and support.

About 10% of women experience a more severe and sustained depressive episode that meets diagnostic criteria for major depression (see pages 32–35). Onset is usually during or after the third week following delivery and duration can be many months. Professional intervention in the form of psychotherapy and antidepressant medication is usually quite helpful.

The most severe form of postpartum mood disorder is a psychosis that occurs in about 1 to 3 per thousand. It often begins shortly after delivery, with 40% of the episodes beginning by day 7. This is a very serious *high-risk* condition characterized by hallucinations, delusions, and confusion that usually requires hospitalization and treatment with medication and sometimes with electroconvulsive therapy (ECT). Although postpartum psychosis has often been misdiagnosed as schizophrenia, it is almost always a form of depressive or manic-depressive disorder.

Overall, women with a history of mood disorder (depression or manic-depression) prior to pregnancy are at greatly increased risk for a postpartum recurrence. Consequently, such problems should be anticipated and proper attention paid to reduction of stressors and the possible preventive use of medication (see page 89 for discussion of medication at the time of conception and during pregnancy). Close collaboration between obstetrician, pediatrician, and mental health professional is essential. There is a national group, Depression After Delivery, that serves as a clearinghouse for information and refers women to local support groups. The address is Depression After Delivery, P.O. Box 1282, Morrisville, PA 19067.

How common is depression in the elderly? Community surveys have found that major depression is actually less prevalent among the elderly than in those under the age of 65. Nonetheless, it is estimated that 1%–2% of the elderly in the community and 10%–20% of those in institutions have major depression. Many more have depression symptoms associated with stressors such as retirement, financial problems, illness, death of friends and family members, and the increasing certainty of their own demise. This combination of genetic and situational factors helps explain the growing numbers of elderly individuals suffering from depression. When these risk factors are added to the increasing number of elderly in our population, it is less surprising that depression is so common in this group. Life expectancy in the United States has increased from 47 years in 1900 to 71 years in men and 78 years in women in 1985. In 1900, the elderly (age 65 and over) made up 4% of the population. Today this figure has increased to 12.7%; by the year 2000, it will be 14%–15%; and by the year 2020 it will reach 18%–20%.

Depression combined with medical illness appears to lead to earlier death in some patients. Attempts at self-treatment of depression by the elderly may lead to alcohol or other drug abuse, just as it may in younger individuals. About 10% of older people thought to be suffering from senile dementias (Alzheimer's and others) are, instead, actually depressed. This "pseudo" or false dementia can be reversed with proper antidepressant drug treatment. Depression may also coexist with senile dementia. Even then proper treatment can be quite helpful.

Elderly individuals suffering from depression respond to the same antidepressant treatments that help younger people, although smaller doses of antidepressant drugs are often effective because metabolism slows with aging.

What role does fatigue play in depression? All problems seem worse when we are tired or fatigued, and a good night's sleep usually puts things into a more realistic perspective. Lady Macbeth properly praised "sleep that knits up the ravell'd sleave of care." With depression, sleep is often difficult and seldom relieves fatigue even if the person sleeps for many hours. The fatigue of depression is unrelieved by rest and sleep, and depressed people must struggle with the continuous burden of fatigue. Antidepressant treatment, not rest or sleep, is the cure for fatigue caused by depression. It is possible, though not certain, that fatigue which builds up as a result of too many pressures or from ignoring our bodies' needs for "good food, fresh air, rest, and exercise—the quadrangle of health" may contribute to the development of depression.

What about chronic fatigue syndrome (CFS)? Much has been written in recent years about a condition characterized by chronic, disabling fatigue. *Newsweek* (November 12, 1990) referred to it as "a modern medical mystery." Although controversy abounds with regard to its cause(s) and treatment(s), most authorities agree that the syndrome exists. Unfortunately, there is no highly accurate diagnostic test for CFS; *Consumer Reports* (October 1990) referred to it as "an illusive epidemic'' and ''a magnet for quacks.'' The symptoms of CFS and depression are quite similar and it is likely that depression is the more appropriate diagnosis for some individuals carrying the label of CFS. In such instances, there is every reason to expect a favorable response to the usual treatments for depression.

Can hypoglycemia cause depression?   Hypoglycemia or low blood sugar can cause emotional symptoms such as anxiety, sweating, shakiness, weakness, lightheadedness, and fatigue. These symptoms, however, are more often due to other causes. Symptoms of depression are only very rarely due to hypoglycemia. The unfortunate tendency to overdiagnose hypoglycemia often results in inappropriate treatment and hides the correct diagnosis. The properly conducted measurement of blood sugar is a necessary part of a hypoglycemia evaluation. Ideally this would involve finding a sufficiently low blood sugar at the time symptoms are present and relieving of symptoms when blood sugar level is restored to normal.

Can allergies cause depression?   Controversy surrounds this issue. Although recent studies have shown that food hypersensitivity can cause psychological symptoms in some people, there have been no conclusive studies that prove that allergy causes depression. A movement known as clinical ecology holds that illnesses (including depression) are often caused by hypersensitivity or ''allergic'' reactions to a wide variety of environmental substances. The mainstream of medicine, however, regards such claims as extravagant and unsubstantiated. Well-designed research studies are needed to resolve this controversy. One such study scientifically tested a group of patients who believed that food allergy caused many of their medical and psychological symptoms. Only 17% actually had hypersensitivity to foods, and none of them had psychological symptoms.

Can hormone imbalance cause depression? *Yes*, but depressive symptoms usually occur as part of a group of other findings that suggest a particular hormonal disorder. Occasionally this is not the case and depression may be the only finding. At other times, depression and a hormonal disorder may occur at the same time but be unrelated.

Hormonal or endocrine disorders that may cause depressive symptoms include thyroid gland underactivity (hypothyroidism) and very rarely overactivity (apathetic hyperthyroidism); underactivity (Addison's disease) or overactivity (Cushing's syndrome) of the adrenal gland; underactivity or overactivity of the parathyroid gland (disordered calcium metabolism); and premenstrual syndrome (PMS). Hormonal drugs such as oral contraceptives (birth control pills) and steroids (cortisone, prednisone, etc.) occasionally cause depressive symptoms.

If depressive symptoms are due to a hormonal abnormality, they will be relieved when the abnormality is corrected. For example, oral contraceptives may cause a depression linked to a deficiency in pyridoxine (vitamin B_6). In such cases, treatment with a low dose of pyridoxine will overcome the depression. A comprehensive evaluation of depression should include attention to the endocrine system.

What is the relationship between premenstrual syndrome (PMS) and depression? The recent explosion of interest in symptoms related to the menstrual cycle has focused much attention on this real but perplexing entity. Despite the emergence of specialty clinics and special interest groups, no consistent definition, cause, or treatment of this syndrome has been developed. In some women, depressive symptoms are limited to the premenstrual phase of the cycle while in others depression is persistent throughout the cycle but aggravated premenstrually. In others, depressive symptoms seem quite independent from and uninfluenced by the menstrual cycle.

To better establish if there is a relationship between mood and menses, some form of a daily rating scale kept over several cycles may be quite helpful. Although there are no well-established, consistently effective treatments for PMS, a variety of treatments are available that have been beneficial in some women. If depression is a prominent aspect of PMS, it may respond to one of these treatment measures (which, incidentally, include antidepressant drugs). It is important that any treatment be conducted in a safe and systematic fashion under the supervision of a doctor experienced in dealing with this disorder.

What can I do to fight depression? It depends. If depression is mild, if other aspects of your life are in good order (relationships, occupation, health, etc.), and if you are able to participate regularly in interpersonal (page 48) or cognitive-behavioral psychotherapy (page 48) or to exercise (page 81) on a regular basis, you may recover from a mild depression. Sometimes depression stops without treatment after enough time has passed, often several months or even a few years. At times with mild depression, usually with moderate depression, and almost always with severe depression, *you will need help* in the form of medication to overcome the depression.

How effective are treatments for depression? Very effective! The first antidepressant medicine you and your doctor try has about a 70% chance of helping. Cognitive and interpersonal psychotherapies may also be effective for less severe depressions. If the first treatment fails, other effective treatments are available. No one has real reason to fear that his or her depression is untreatable.

Are antidepressant medicines the same as tranquilizers, pep pills, "uppers," sleeping pills, pain pills, sex pills, or nerve pills? *NO!* Antidepressant medicines stand in a class by themselves. Antidepressant medications counteract anxiety, pain, decreased energy, loss of sex drive, and sleep disturbance, but do so by treating the underlying depression that causes all of these symptoms. In this way, the body's normal functioning is restored. And it's important to remember that antidepressant medications do not cause addiction, a concern expressed by some patients and members of their families.

Am I Depressed?

Everyone has unpleasant experiences that can lead to feelings of sadness or the blues. Most of these feelings are short-lived and go away when the unpleasant experiences stop or when better ways of dealing with problems are found. The boundary line between normal blues or sadness and depression that requires treatment is not sharply defined. Some patients seek treatment for sadness that would disappear spontaneously in a few days. Some physicians withhold treatment until they are absolutely certain that depression is present. These different boundary lines for deciding when to seek and to offer treatment are understandable considering our current incomplete knowledge about depression.

Most professionals agree that depression should be treated if it causes sustained interference in general social activities, intimate relationships, or educational or occupational functioning. Many agree that treatment should be considered when personal suffering from depression reaches a distressing level for the individual even though he or she is able to handle most life situations. In the end, decisions regarding the need to treat depression are best made on individual grounds by patient and doctor. Severe depression may seriously impair judgment and decision-making ability. The hopelessness caused by depression may discourage a patient from pursuing treatment that would otherwise be effective. When disagreements arise, involvement of the family, a second opinion from another doctor, or the passage of time may relieve the uncertainty.

If we accept that disagreements remain about *defining* and *diagnosing* depression, what help is available for *identifying* depression? A number of self-report, paper-and-pencil questionnaires have been developed to help with general screening for depression. These include the Beck Depression Inventory, the Zung Self-Rating Depression Scale, and the Wakefield Self-Report Questionnaire.

The Hamilton Depression Rating Scale, which was developed by Max Hamilton in the 1950s, has become the recognized standard for rating severity and change in depressive symptoms. Unfortunately, it requires that a clinician observe a patient and complete the rating instrument. More recently, the Wakefield Self-Report Questionnaire was developed at the Wakefield Hospital in 1971, where Dr. Hamilton and his colleagues practiced. Dr. R. P. Snaith played the lead role in development and study of the Wakefield questionnaire, and it is reproduced here with his kind permission. This questionnaire permits people who may be depressed to obtain a depression rating score by answering 12 simple questions.

Wakefield Self-Report Questionnaire

Read these statements carefully, one at a time, and underline or circle the response that best indicates how you are. It is most important to indicate *how you are now*, not how you were, or how you would hope to be.

A. I feel miserable and sad.
   0) No, not at all
   1) No, not much
   2) Yes, sometimes
   3) Yes, definitely

B. I find it easy to do the things I used to do.
   0) Yes, definitely
   1) Yes, sometimes
   2) No, not much
   3) No, not at all

C. I get very frightened or panicky feeling for apparently no reason at all.
   0) No, not at all
   1) No, not much
   2) Yes, sometimes
   3) Yes, definitely

D. I have weeping spells, or feel like it.
   0) No, not at all
   1) No, not much
   2) Yes, sometimes
   3) Yes, definitely

E. I still enjoy the things I used to.
    0) Yes, definitely
    1) Yes, sometimes
    2) No, not much
    3) No, not at all

F. I am restless and can't keep still.
    0) No, not at all
    1) No, not much
    2) Yes, sometimes
    3) Yes, definitely

G. I get off to sleep easily without sleeping tablets.
    0) Yes, definitely
    1) Yes, sometimes
    2) No, not much
    3) No, not at all

H. I feel anxious when I go out of the house on my own.
    0) No, not at all
    1) No, not much
    2) Yes, sometimes
    3) Yes, definitely

I. I have lost interest in things.
    0) No, not at all
    1) No, not much
    2) Yes, sometimes
    3) Yes, definitely

J. I get tired for no reason.
    0) No, not at all
    1) No, not much

2) Yes, sometimes
3) Yes, definitely

K. I am more irritable than usual.
   0) No, not at all
   1) No, not much
   2) Yes, sometimes
   3) Yes, definitely

L. I wake early and then sleep badly for the rest of the night.
   0) No, not at all
   1) No, not much
   2) Yes, sometimes
   3) Yes, definitely

The Wakefield Self-Report Questionnaire is scored by adding up the numbers selected for each of the 12 items. Most depressed people tend to score above 14 on the Wakefield, whereas most nondepressed people score between 0 and 14. It is important to realize that a rating scale such as the Wakefield does not diagnose clinical depression but is instead a measure of symptoms often associated with depression. It is likely that high scores may also be attained by individuals with other emotional problems or physical illnesses. Therefore, use the test as a guide, and consider consulting a doctor for an evaluation if your score is high.

Scores lower than 15 may still warrant consultation with a doctor if your distress or dysfunction is substantial. Repeating the Wakefield approximately 2 weeks after its first use may be helpful, and if your score is rising, you should strongly consider consulting a doctor.

It is important not to depend too heavily on outside measures of depression. Although they can add some objectivity to the assessment of depression and permit comparisons with a large population of individuals with depression, *the subjective experience of depression* is highly variable. Some people with normal scores on a depression questionnaire are severely depressed and respond dramatically to treatment.

Diagnosis and DSM-III-R

Questionnaires are *not diagnostic of depression* but are helpful as screening devices. Diagnoses of depression are now made on the basis of criteria contained in the *Diagnostic and Statistical Manual of Mental Disorders*, *Third Edition*, *Revised* (DSM-III-R) of the American Psychiatric Association (APA; 1987). DSM-III-R is designed for *use by clinicians* and was not written for patients. Although we list various depressive disorders as defined by DSM-III-R in the Appendix of this book, we feel it is helpful for patients to see an example of the criteria of one kind of depression, namely *major depression*, which is the common diagnosis for depression requiring treatment. The criteria, reproduced with permission of the APA, are as follows:

Diagnostic Criteria
for Major Depressive Episode

Note: A "Major Depressive Syndrome" is defined as criterion A below.

A. At least five of the following symptoms have been present during the same two-week period and represent a change from previous functioning; at least one of the symptoms is either (1) depressed mood, or (2) loss of interest or pleasure. (Do not include symptoms that are clearly due to a physical condition, mood-incongruent delusions or hallucinations, incoherence, or marked loosening of associations.)

(1) depressed mood (or can be irritable mood in children and adolescents) most of the day, nearly every day, as indicated either by subjective account or observation by others

(2) markedly diminished interest or pleasure in all, or almost all, activities most of the day, nearly every day (as indicated either by subjective account or observation by others of apathy most of the time)

(3) significant weight loss or weight gain when not dieting (e.g., more than 5% of body weight in a month), or decrease or increase in appetite nearly every day (in children, consider failure to make expected weight gains)

(4) insomnia or hypersomnia nearly every day

(5) psychomotor agitation or retardation nearly every day (observable by others, not merely subjective feelings of restlessness or being slowed down)

(6) fatigue or loss of energy nearly every day

(7) feelings of worthlessness or excessive or inappropriate guilt (which may be delusional) nearly every day (not merely self-reproach or guilt about being sick)

(8) diminished ability to think or concentrate, or indecisiveness, nearly every day (either by subjective account or as observed by others)

(9) recurrent thoughts of death (not just fear of dying), recurrent suicidal ideation without a specific plan, or a suicide attempt or a specific plan for committing suicide

B. (1) It cannot be established that an organic factor initiated and maintained the disturbance.
   (2) The disturbance is not a normal reaction to the death of a loved one (Uncomplicated Bereavement).

Note: Morbid preoccupation with worthlessness, suicidal ideation, marked functional impairment or psychomotor retardation, or prolonged duration suggest bereavement complicated by Major Depression.

C. At no time during the disturbance have there been delusions or hallucinations for as long as two weeks in the absence of prominent mood symptoms (i.e., before the mood symptoms developed or after they have remitted).

D. Not superimposed on Schizophrenia, Schizophreniform Disorder, Delusional Disorder, or Psychotic Disorder NOS.

Major Depressive Episode codes: fifth-digit code numbers and criteria for severity of current state of Bipolar Disorder, Depressed, or Major Depression:

1—Mild: Few, if any, symptoms in excess of those required to make the diagnosis, **and** symptoms result in only minor impairment in occupational functioning or in usual social activities or relationships with others.

2—Moderate: Symptoms or functional impairment between "mild" and "severe."

3—Severe, without Psychotic Features: Several symptoms in excess of those required to make the diagnosis, **and** symptoms markedly interfere with occupational functioning or with usual social activities or relationships with others.

4—With Psychotic Features: Delusions or hallucinations. If possible, **specify** whether the psychotic features are mood-congruent or mood-incongruent.

Mood-congruent psychotic features: Delusions or hallucinations whose content is entirely consistent with the typical depressive themes of personal inadequacy, guilt, disease, death, nihilism, or deserved punishment.

Mood-incongruent psychotic features: Delusions or hallucinations whose content does not involve typical depressive themes of personal inadequacy, guilt, disease, death, nihilism, or deserved punishment. Included here are such symptoms as persecutory delusions (not directly related to depressive themes), thought insertion, thought broadcasting, and delusions of control.

5—In Partial Remission: Intermediate between "In Full Remission" and "Mild," **and** no previous Dysthymia. (If Major Depressive Episode was superimposed on Dysthymia, the diagnosis of Dysthymia alone is given once the full criteria for a Major Depressive Episode are no longer met.)

6—In Full Remission: During the past six months no significant signs or symptoms of the disturbance.

0—Unspecified.

Specify chronic if current episode has lasted two consecutive years without a period of two months or longer during which there were no significant depressive symptoms.

Specify if current episode is **Melancholic Type**.

Other depressive disorders defined in DSM-III-R are: Bipolar Disorder (manic-depression), Cyclothymia, Dysthymia, Schizoaffective Disorder, Adjustment Disorder with Depressed Mood, Uncomplicated Bereavement, Organic Mood Disorder, Dementia with Depression, Substance-induced Mood Disorder, Bipolar Disorder Not Otherwise Specified and Depressive Disorder Not Otherwise Specified. Each disorder has specific criteria for diagnosis (see Appendix) and the process of diagnosis when done properly is quite complicated.

Diagnosis clearly requires careful consideration of many factors including the individual's history, family history, response to treatment, and present symptoms (what patients complain of) and signs (what doctors and others observe). The increasing complexity of psychiatric diagnosis is providing improved diagnostic accuracy. An open mind, strong powers of observation, continuing study of diagnostic advances, patience, and experience combine to make an excellent diagnostician. If the diagnosis is not clear or if the response to treatment is less than satisfactory, both patient and doctor may benefit from a consultation or second opinion.

Laboratory Tests

Several new laboratory tests to identify depression are being evaluated. These tests attempt to identify markers of abnormalities in biological function that suggest a likelihood of depression. Blood, urine, and sometimes spinal fluid or skin are used in these tests. Measurement of brain "waves" or electrical activity by electroencephalogram (EEG) and brain structure with computed tomography (CT) or magnetic resonance imaging (MRI) is also being studied. Brain metabolism can also be assessed in some research settings with techniques called positron-emission tomography (PET) and single photon emission computed tomography (SPECT). Despite much promising research being conducted in these areas, there are currently no laboratory tests that can reliably diagnose depression, predict the best treatment, or predict the response of a given individual to any particular treatment.

All of these tests remain under development. However, one—the dexamethasone suppression test (DST or DEX test)—has reached a stage of development where some psychiatrists are using it with some of their patients. The test measures the change in blood levels of cortisol following a dose of dexamethasone, a potent steroid hormone. However, in about half of people with major depression, the DST is normal and these individuals usually respond as well to standard antidepressant medications as do those who have abnormal DSTs. Also, the DST is sometimes abnormal, even in the absence of depression.

Although laboratory tests cannot be reliably used to diagnose depression, they may play an important role in the overall evaluation of depressed patients. This is especially true when searching for associated medical illness that may contribute to or occasionally cause depression.

While you are being treated with an antidepressant, your doctor may want to measure the amount of the drug in your blood. This is done to ensure that the dose you are taking is producing a safe and therapeutic blood level. Many doctors, however, treat most of their patients quite effectively without the routine use of blood levels. Also, there continues to be controversy over what constitutes a "therapeutic level" for many of the antidepressants. As these issues are clarified, we expect to see more extensive use being made of these tests.

Summary

A diagnosis of depression rests on a careful history of present symptoms and past episodes, family history, observations of the patient by the physician (including physical examination), reports of family members, and laboratory studies. *All of these factors must be weighed* in the process of coming to a decision about diagnosis and the need for treatment. At times, the diagnosis may be unclear and a further period of observation may be needed. At other times when the diagnosis is unclear, patient and doctor may decide to begin treatment because distress is of such magnitude that waiting is unjustified.

With the development of questionnaires, diagnostic systems such as DSM-III-R, and great strides in the fields of epidemiology (study of the frequency and distribution of disorders), basic science, laboratory testing, and clinical research, both diagnosis and treatment of depression are becoming more refined and successful.

What About Suicide?

ach year, suicide accounts for at least 25,000 deaths (12 out of every 100,000 persons) in the United States. This figure may represent a substantial underreporting because some suicides appear to be accidents and because of the social stigma attached to suicide or the possible loss of insurance benefits. Some experts estimate that as many as 75,000 people commit suicide each year. Suicide is the major cause of premature death in psychiatric patients, and about three-quarters of those who commit suicide do so while depressed. Risk of suicide is greater in men than in women, although women make more suicide attempts. Suicide risk increases with age, but suicide is the second or third leading cause of death for young people. Although the suicide rate among young people is lower than in some other age groups, the number of suicides among 15- to 24-year-olds has *tripled* in the last 25 to 30 years.

Prediction of suicide risk remains a difficult problem. Even individuals with all of the most powerful predictors of suicide risk have only a 5% probability of committing suicide in the next year. Nevertheless, this risk is 500 times greater than in the population at large.

Depressed persons and those around them must be aware of the risk of suicide. The old saw about "people who talk about suicide never do it" is simply not true. Thoughts of suicide are common during depression, and people with these distressing thoughts will often share them with those they trust. Some individuals, however, keep such thoughts to themselves. Asking about such concerns may seem awkward but it is an essential aspect of evaluating depression. When a person shares thoughts of self-injury or suicide, an assessment of suicide risk should be made by a professional as soon as possible. Most of the time, patients with suicidal thoughts do not require hospitalization, but sometimes hospitalization is appropriate to reduce the risk of suicide.

The factors listed below have the greatest *statistical* accuracy in predicting suicide risk. Statistical averages are difficult to apply to individuals because at times unusual factors are involved in an individual's decision to attempt suicide.

1. **Age**. In the United States, the suicide rate in white males increases with age, and in 1982 the rate for those 75 years and older was twice that of 45- to 54-year-olds. In contrast, suicide rates for black males do not increase with age; in fact, the rate is highest in 25- to 34-year-olds. Rates for women tend to increase to age 60 or so and then decrease.

Those over 65 make up about 12% of the population but account for about 17% of all suicides.

2. **Sex**. Males are three to four times more likely to die from a suicide attempt than females, but females make three to four times as many attempts as males.

3. **Depression**. About three-quarters of the people who kill themselves are depressed at the time they do so. Feelings of helplessness, hopelessness or worthlessness, or guilt about some real or imagined fault often lead to thoughts of suicide. At least 10% of people with major depression end their lives by suicide.

4. **Previous suicide attempt**. Sixty percent of people who kill themselves have made a previous suicide attempt.

5. **Alcohol or other drug abuse**. Alcohol is the most widely available and most abused drug in our society. Alcohol and other drug abuse sometimes reflects attempts at self-treatment of depression with drugs. Suicide may be precipitated by discouragement that comes with a life complicated by drugs as well as confusion and loss of control associated with intoxication.

6. **Recent loss of important persons, positions, or possessions**. This includes death or separation because of divorce, loss of a job whether through discharge or retirement, and loss of prized possessions.

7. **Social isolation**. People living alone and without support of friends.

8. **Beginnings of recovery** from depression with renewed energy and determination in a person with previous thoughts of suicide.

9. **Clear plans** for committing suicide with a method that is likely to be lethal, and access to the instruments of suicide.

Summary

Depressed persons and those around them must be aware of the risk of suicide. The old saw about "people who talk about suicide never do it" is simply not true. Thoughts of suicide are common during depression and people with these distressing thoughts will often share them with those they trust. When a patient shares thoughts of self-injury or suicide, an assessment of suicide risk should be made by a professional. Most of the time, patients with suicidal thoughts can remain outpatients. Sometimes hospitalization is appropriate to reduce the risk of suicide.

How Is Depression Treated?

Just as there are different factors that may cause depression, there are different treatments for depression. Sometimes these treatments are aimed directly at the presumed causes of depression. More often they are given because they have been shown to be generally helpful or because the doctor is most familiar with their use.

Psychotherapy (talk therapy) is always appropriate for depression that requires treatment. There are various types of psychotherapy ranging from supportive psychotherapy to those with the more ambitious goals of effectively alleviating symptoms of depression, uncovering psychological causes of depression, and helping the patient to insights and changes in personality characteristics and behaviors that may prevent recurrence of depression. See pages 45–52 for further information on psychotherapy.

Medications are the cornerstone of treatment for major depressions. The effectiveness of antidepressant medications has been conclusively proven, but issues of selecting the best medication and minimizing side effects remain important. Pages 53–76 cover medications in more detail.

Electroconvulsive therapy (ECT) has been maligned in recent years. However, ECT remains the single most effective treatment for severe depression, is most effective in lessening or eliminating suicidal risk, and is sometimes helpful when other treatments have failed. ECT is described more fully on pages 77–79.

Other treatments such as exercise, sleep deprivation, light therapy, and psychosurgery are controversial and the subject of ongoing research. Each of these treatments appears to be useful for some patients. Please see pages 81–84 for more information.

All of the treatments mentioned in this chapter have a role to play in the treatment of depression. Selecting the best treatment for each patient requires knowledge, experience, skill, and sometimes luck. When one treatment is ineffective, it is likely that another will be successful. Optimism that a successful treatment will be found, persistence in pursuit of a successful treatment, and flexibility in matching patient with treatment are hallmarks of good treatment of depression. Each of these classes of treatment will be discussed in more detail in the following chapters.

Psychotherapy

Psychotherapy is sometimes referred to as "talk" therapy. Patients and their doctors talk about the experiences patients have had and are having, important relationships, and future goals, as well as the feelings, thoughts, and behaviors they produce. Psychotherapies are usually most helpful for less severe depressions, which form the largest part of the depressive spectrum. Psychotherapies alone are less effective for more severe depressions, but may be helpful in improving relationships, thinking patterns, or behaviors that may have led to depression. General support of depressed patients is always beneficial and may sustain them through their suffering even if other treatments are ineffective. Education about depression and its treatment is an important part of all psychotherapies.

Although psychotherapies are frequently provided to depressed patients, and many clinicians believe in their usefulness, there have been fewer scientific studies of their effectiveness compared with the studies of the effectiveness of antidepressant medications and electroconvulsive therapy. There are scores of specific named psychotherapies. However, most psychotherapies are variations on one of the following five approaches.

Supportive Psychotherapy

All patients need and deserve support and empathic understanding while they are depressed. Supportive psychotherapy helps by shoring up defenses, utilizing strengths, empathizing with distress, explaining the course of depression, monitoring changes, and reassuring the patient that improvement will, in time, occur. It also helps the doctor learn the effects of other treatments from the patient. With the patient's permission, support and explanation should also be provided to family members, friends, and others important in the patient's life. These individuals constitute a network of support more available than anything the doctor can provide. When other treatments are ineffective, support by caring others can sustain a person until depression resolves on its own with the passage of time. All doctors provide support to their patients. Family doctors often know patients best and are, therefore, a most important source of support.

Dynamic Psychotherapy

Dynamic therapies seek to understand unresolved unconscious conflicts that may lead to depression. Depression is often described as anger turned inward, and it is felt that helping the individual uncover, understand, and deal more appropriately with angry feelings may lead to recovery from depression. Interpretation of dreams, free association, and exploration of the past are important techniques of psychoanalytic psychotherapy. Other psychodynamic psychotherapists may use the same techniques but focus more on present relationships and role functioning. Patients are helped to understand the possible role of these factors in their depression and to find new ways of dealing with people and feelings. Dynamic psychotherapy may continue for periods ranging from a few months to several years.

Short-Term Therapies

By definition, short-term therapies are limited in length. They often last from a few weeks to several months (commonly 10 to 20 sessions), focus more on the present rather than the past, and usually involve an active collaboration between patient and therapist. Patients are encouraged to put forward their view of the problems they face and the therapist explores alternative explanations in a warm, interested, and respectful manner. Other common characteristics of short-term therapies include defining concrete and measurable targets for treatment, setting modest and achievable goals before progressing to more difficult problems, identifying and correcting obvious deficiencies such as poor anger control and lack of assertiveness, and regularly providing feedback regarding problems and progress in therapy. Three short-term therapies have shown effectiveness in careful research studies.

Interpersonal Psychotherapy

This approach uses both supportive and dynamic psychotherapeutic techniques. Because depression occurs in the context of relationships (poor relationships may lead to depression and depression may damage relationships), emphasis is placed on understanding and improving the relationship skills of the patient. Goals are to reduce depressive symptoms, improve self-esteem, and help the patient develop new strategies for improving social and interpersonal functioning. Individuals with ingrained and severe personality problems would usually not be treated with interpersonal psychotherapy. Specific techniques are available to help with problems of grief, role changes, interpersonal disputes, and deficits the patient may have in interpersonal functioning. Both short- and long-term scientific studies have found beneficial effects from the use of interpersonal psychotherapy to treat depression. There is some evidence that combining interpersonal psychotherapy with antidepressant medication offers further advantages.

Cognitive-Behavioral Therapy

Cognitive-behavioral therapists help patients by focusing on their negative "cognitions" or thoughts about themselves, the world, and the future. Negative thoughts about oneself lead to lowered self-esteem; depressed people often feel defective and lacking in positive attributes that they believe everyone else has in abundance. Negative thoughts about the world lead to excessive caution and guardedness; those who are depressed view the glass as "half empty" and describe life as demanding and depriving. Typically, they place a negative interpretation on ambiguous events that others would view more neutrally or even positively. Negative thoughts about the future lead to pessimism and hopelessness; when depressed, many are convinced that the feelings they have will continue forever and that they deserve this fate. Cognitive therapists believe that these negative thoughts can precipitate and perpetuate depression.

To understand the cognitive perspective on depression, you might conduct an exercise of immersing yourself in consistently negative cognitions for 5 minutes to determine what effect this process has on your mood. Most people find the experience somewhat depressing and can understand how a preoccupation with such pessimistic themes can contribute to depression. Specific educational, cognitive, and behavioral techniques have been combined to counteract the negative thoughts so common in depression and the behaviors that result from negative thinking. Usually, behaviors are changed first before focused work begins on cognitions or thoughts, which, in turn, precedes improvements in mood. For example, an individual who reports "I can't do anything," when asked to be more specific might offer, "I used to love to cook but now I have no interest in cooking and couldn't even take the first step if I did. I feel useless and know I'll never feel better." The cognitive-behavioral therapist would seek this patient's agreement to initiate a graded task assignment requiring a tiny behavior such as "boiling water." This behavioral step must be taken without sarcasm and with empathy for the distress the patient is experiencing, and the difficulty such a seemingly simple task may represent for this patient. A number of scientific studies have shown a beneficial effect of cognitive therapy in treating mild to moderately severe depression. Cognitive therapy does not appear to be effective for severe depression.

The National Institute of Mental Health has supported a multicenter study of the effectiveness of well-trained therapists providing interpersonal psychotherapy or cognitive-behavioral therapy or imipramine (a tricyclic antidepressant) or placebo (an inactive substance). Results indicate that both interpersonal psychotherapy and imipramine were effective in the treatment of mild, moderate, and severe depression. However, "severe," as defined in this study, did not include the most severely depressed patients, who were thought so unlikely to respond to psychotherapy that they were excluded.

Cognitive-behavioral therapy produced significant improvement for patients with mild or moderate depression but not those suffering "severe" depression.

Interestingly, even the placebo treatment produced significant improvement although fewer placebo patients recovered fully. The explanation for this finding may lie in the supportive contact the patients received from the doctors who were monitoring their placebo medication. Overall, patients who received either type of psychotherapy or imipramine showed trends toward better outcome at the end of treatment than patients who received placebo. However, the differences between the patients who received treatment and those receiving placebo "were often not statistically significant, especially for the psychotherapies." Also, the benefit from the psychotherapies, especially for cognitive-behavioral therapy, was less consistent than for treatment with imipramine. This means that the matching of patient and psychotherapist has an effect on outcome, which is not as much of an issue when imipramine, a medication, is the main treatment.

Behavior Therapy

Depressed patients have changes in their behaviors, and behavior therapy attempts to alleviate depression by returning behavior patterns toward normal. This approach helps patients increase the number of normal and nondepressed behaviors so that they will receive the positive reinforcements from thoughts and feelings associated with more normal behavior patterns. Behavioral techniques are used to increase enjoyable activities, decrease or minimize the effects of unpleasant events, increase rewards for achieving goals, enhance social skills, use time more effectively and efficiently, and develop cognitive approaches similar to those used in formal cognitive therapy.

Because there are so many components of behavioral therapy of depression, it is difficult to arrive at firm conclusions about the effectiveness of behavior therapy as a whole. Nevertheless, most studies have indicated that behavior therapy of depression is superior to no treatment.

Summary

Whatever else happens in psychotherapy, the patient is provided with a relationship with a doctor who has worked with other depressed patients. Through this relationship the therapist provides information about depression and support to patient and family. Psychotherapists also engender hope by providing an explanation for depression and help in pursuing a particular psychotherapeutic approach to the relief of depression.

Final conclusions about the relative effectiveness of psychotherapy and medications for different kinds of depression await further carefully controlled studies. At present, our understanding of the available research suggests:

1. Mild and moderate depression account for about two-thirds of all depression.
2. Although mild depression often disappears without treatment, it may stop sooner with psychotherapy. Mild depression that is long-lasting or unresponsive to psychotherapy may be helped by medication.
3. Moderate and severe depressions usually require treatment with antidepressant medications, which are commonly given in conjunction with psychotherapy. The combination of interpersonal or cognitive therapy with antidepressant medications may be more effective than either treatment alone for moderate depression. Severe depression is unlikely to respond to psychotherapy and should not be treated solely with psychotherapy. Antidepressant medications and electroconvulsive therapy (supplemented with psychotherapy) are critical to the effective treatment of severe depression.
4. Psychotherapy and medication should not be seen as competitive but, rather, as compatible and complementary. Medications are most effective in relieving symptoms of depression while those psychotherapies that have been shown to be effective *may* help patients change aspects of their thinking and ways of relating that make them more vulnerable to depression.

Antidepressant
Medications

Introduction

Antidepressant medications are the cornerstone of treatment of major depression and often play a role in the treatment of less severe depression. Indications for the use of antidepressant medications are usually straightforward and involve the presence of depressive mood, thoughts, behaviors, and physical symptoms (as described on pages 1–3 and 32–35).

Sometimes depressions are hidden or ''masked''—patients may complain of pain such as headache, backache, or stomachache instead of sadness; or they may insist that they feel fine, but fail to go to work or look quite upset; or they may first notice panic attacks or phobias (fears they recognize as unreasonable); or they may become obsessed with fears or pestered by compulsive rituals; or they may abuse alcohol or other drugs in attempts at self-treatment of depression. Depression may also be signaled by other "atypical" physical or emotional complaints.

The accurate diagnosis of depression is a necessary step in the process of selecting appropriate medications or other treatments. A thorough history is essential and a physical examination and laboratory tests are often necessary to select the best treatment for depression. The clinician should consider the patient's past history of depression and response to earlier treatments, family history of depression and treatment response, concurrent medical problems and their treatments, occupational and social impairment, severity of depression, risk of suicide, age, importance of speedy recovery, patient reliability, and preference for treatment.

Several different classes of antidepressant medications are available. *Tricyclic* antidepressants and newer drugs with different chemical structures but similar effectiveness are the major antidepressant medications. They are often referred to as *cyclic antidepressants* because they contain one or more cyclic rings in their structure (a tricyclic has 3 such rings). *Monoamine oxidase inhibitors* (MAOIs) make up the other main class of medications for treatment of depression. (Strictly speaking, they too are cyclic structures, but other properties cause them to be classified separately.) *Lithium*, used primarily in the treatment of mania and depression when those two disorders occur together or in sequence, may also be effective in cases where depression is the only problem. A number of other medications are sometimes added to the three main classes of medication (cyclic antidepressants, MAOIs, and lithium). They will be discussed on pages 74–76.

Antidepressant medications are generally safe and effective

when used as directed. But all medications are double-edged swords with unwanted side effects as well as beneficial main effects. Most antidepressant side effects are minor annoyances and many side effects decrease in severity as patients' bodies grow accustomed to the medication. When depression is treated with medications, there is almost always some minor cost in terms of side effects to pay for the major benefit of relief of depression. Keeping the costs low and the benefits high is important and can almost always be accomplished in a cooperative relationship between patient and doctor.

Most major depressions respond to treatment with the first antidepressant medication. If the first medication seems ineffective, it is important to make certain that it has been given in sufficient dose and for a sufficient period of time. Undertreatment is a common cause of treatment failure.

If the first medication fails, it is common practice to try a second medication unless there is reason to switch to electroconvulsive therapy (ECT) for prompt relief of severe depression. Second medications may be from the same drug class or a shift may be made to another class of medication (for example, from tricyclics to MAOIs or lithium). If a second drug has failed to relieve depression (particularly if it is from a different class of antidepressant medications), combinations of antidepressants may be tried. Rather than immediately switching to a different antidepressant if the first is ineffective, some physicians prefer to add a second drug (often lithium or thyroid hormone) to the first—a procedure known as "augmentation."

Depression that reaches psychotic proportions (when a person exhibits delusions and/or hallucinations and has clearly lost contact with reality) usually requires treatment with either electroconvulsive therapy (ECT) or an antidepressant medication plus an antipsychotic drug such as chlorpromazine (Thorazine), haloperidol (Haldol), or thiothixene (Navane). The only antidepressant with acceptable effectiveness against psychotic depression when used alone is amoxapine (Asendin).

Cyclic Antidepressants (Unicyclics, Bicyclics, Tricyclics, and Tetracyclics)

Cyclic antidepressants are so named because chemically they contain one or more cyclic or ring structures. The oldest and best established contain 3 fused cyclic structures and are known as tricyclics. The first tricyclic, imipramine (Tofranil, Janimine, SK-Pramine), was introduced in 1958. Amitriptyline (Elavil, Endep, Amitid) was released shortly after. Subsequently, 6 other tricyclics have been marketed in the United States for treating depression. More recently, structurally different (nontricyclic) antidepressants have appeared. These include unicyclics such as bupropion (Wellbutrin) and fluoxetine (Prozac), bicyclics such as sertraline (Zoloft) and trazodone (Desyrel), and the tetracyclic maprotiline (Ludiomil). Other antidepressant medications will be approved for use in the United States in the next few years, and still others are available in other countries but not here.

Large research studies have shown similar effectiveness among all of these drugs in treating major depression. A particular individual, however, may respond to one and not to another, although this is usually not predictable. Certain types of depression (psychotic, atypical, bipolar) may respond better to a particular drug. Antidepressant medications differ in the side effects they may cause and this may suggest the use of one medication over another in a particular individual. Table 1 lists the commonly available cyclic antidepressant

TABLE 1. Cyclic antidepressant medicines

Agent Generic name	Trade name	Usual daily starting dose* (mg)	Usual effective daily dose* (mg)	Relative sedative effects	Relative anticholinergic effects	Relative hypotensive effects
Tricyclic antidepressants						
amitriptyline	Endep Elavil Amiti	50–75	150–300	High	High	More
amoxapine	Asendin	50 three times daily	150–400	Medium	Low	Less
desipramine	Norpramin Pertofrane	50	100–300	Low	Low	More
doxepin	Sinequan	50–75	75–300	High	Medium	More
imipramine	Janimine SK-Pramine Tofranil	50–75	150–300	Medium	Medium	More
nortriptyline	Aventyl Pamelor	25–50	50–100	Low	Medium	Less
protriptyline	Vivactil	5 three times daily	15–60	Low	High	More
trimipramine	Surmontil	50–75	50–200	High	Medium	More
Other antidepressants						
bupropion	Wellbutrin	75–100 twice daily	300–450	Low	Low	Little–None
fluoxetine	Prozac	20	20–80	Low	Low	Little–None
maprotiline	Ludiomil	50–75	125–225	Medium	Low	Less
sertraline	Zoloft	50	50–200	Low	Low	Little–None
trazodone	Desyrel	50 three times daily	150–400	High	Low	Less

*Lower doses (often 1/3 to 1/2 of the usual dose) are used with older patients.

57

medicines and some of the side effects to be considered in their use.

Common side effects from these medications fall into three general classes: sedation (drowsiness or sleepiness); anti-cholinergic effects (dry mouth, blurred vision, constipation, difficulty urinating, increased heart rate, and memory impairment are common examples); and orthostatic hypotension (light-headedness or dizziness when rising from a sitting or lying position). Table 1 lists the severity of these three classes of side effects.

Doses listed in Table 1 are rough guides. Smaller doses are sometimes effective, and larger doses are sometimes necessary. Flexibility is essential.

Less information is available for some of the drugs regarding hypotensive side effects, so we have chosen to use the terms "More," "Less," and "Little–None" rather than the "Low," "Medium," and "High" distinctions for other side effects.

Remember that many patients do well with medications listed as having "High" or "More" side effects. These relative side effect distinctions are presented in Table 1 to make it clear that if side effects are a problem, alternative medications are available.

Many of these medications can be taken as a single dose at bedtime, whereas others require divided dosing and one (fluoxetine) is usually given as a single morning dose. With bedtime dosing, many side effects occur while the patient is asleep. If a single bedtime dose causes problems such as sleepiness the next morning, the medication may be taken at dinnertime or shortly thereafter. For some people, divided doses work best, even for medications that are usually given in a single dose. The doctor may vary the schedule for taking the medication to find the best possible approach for any particular patient. There is no evidence that when an antidepressant is taken during the day is related to its effectiveness.

All of the antidepressant medications shown in Table 1 are effective in the same percentage of people. However, a given individual may benefit from one antidepressant and not from another. Because it is currently impossible to predict which drug will help a particular person (although certain types of depression may show selective responsiveness), minimizing side effects may be the determining factor in selecting the most appropriate drug.

Side Effects

Individuals who must remain alert might be given an antidepressant with low sedative effect. Those who have trouble sleeping are often given a more sedating antidepressant to take at bedtime.

Older patients are more likely to be troubled with anticholinergic effects and may be given a medication less likely to cause those problems. The main anticholinergic side effects are dry mouth, palpitations (rapid and/or uneven heart beat), difficulty urinating, constipation, blurred vision, and memory difficulties.

Patients who experience lightheadedness or dizziness when arising from lying down or sitting positions might be given drugs low in hypotensive (low blood pressure) side effects.

Skin rash, weight gain or loss, restlessness, sweating, agitation, mild shaking (tremor), insomnia, nausea, headache, and many other side effects can occur but do so infrequently. Any unusual experiences while taking an antidepressant medication could be side effects and should be reported to the physician.

Each antidepressant medication can be characterized, in part, by its side effect "profile." Some are very similar while others are quite different; none are identical. Because a particular drug is characterized by certain side effects, it does not mean that an individual will experience them. In fact, most side effects do not occur or if they do, they are easily tolerated. Sometimes, however, intolerable side effects do occur and if so, switching to a drug with a different "profile" will help.

Physician familiarity with a particular medication and its side effects may be the single most important factor recommending its use. Few physicians can truly master the use of all antidepressant medications, and many wise physicians will stick with their familiar favorites unless their patients fail to improve.

Questions About
Cyclic Antidepressants

How long will it take to feel better?   Antidepressants do not work immediately. Several days and often several weeks may pass before they become effective. It is unfortunate that the benefit is delayed, especially since side effects may begin right away. It is important not to get discouraged and give up on the medication or take extra amounts of medication on your own to try to get better faster.

Should I take an antidepressant medication just when I feel depressed?   *NO!* To be effective, antidepressants must be taken *regularly* until depression lifts, and then they are usually continued for 4 months to a year to prevent relapse of the depression. Depression usually begins to lift in 7 to 14 days—sometimes sooner, sometimes later.

People who feel less "depressed" right after they start taking an antidepressant are probably noticing the sedative side effect that many of these medications have. Sedation can relieve anxiety and insomnia, which are frequently part of depression. Sometimes rapid improvements are coincidental with, rather than due to, an antidepressant.

How much medication will I take? There are general guidelines for effective doses (see Table 1 on page 57) and your doctor will usually follow them to begin treatment. However, people's bodies absorb, handle, and excrete these drugs quite differently and two individuals given the same dose may have as much as a 30-fold difference in blood level. Consequently, different patients may require different amounts of a drug to achieve the same benefit.

How does the doctor know the right amount of drug to give me? Aside from general guidelines, you and your doctor will monitor the symptoms and signs of depression for indications that the depression is beginning to lift. Sleep is often one of the first improvements patients notice, followed by improved appetite and later by reversal of pessimism and return of normal energy levels. Sometimes side effects become so severe that an adequate dose of a particular drug cannot be given. Then, switching to another drug is appropriate. Sometimes measuring the blood level of antidepressant drugs is helpful in determining if an inadequate dose is being given or if side effects are caused by unusually high blood levels.

How do antidepressants work? Although the exact reasons that antidepressants relieve depression remain unknown, much has been learned in recent years to support the concept that they correct a "chemical imbalance" in the brain. Neurotransmitters are brain chemicals (sometimes called brain messengers) that are essential for the transmission of information from nerve cell to nerve cell. There is evidence that imbalances or dysregulation of certain neurotransmitters such as serotonin and norepinephrine are related to depression, and that antidepressant drugs work by rebalancing or reregulating these abnormalities. Because some of the newer antidepressants such as fluoxetine (Prozac) and sertraline (Zoloft) specifically affect serotonin, considerable focus has been placed on "serotonin theories" of depression. That this is an oversimplification should be apparent because other drugs such as desipramine (Norpramin, Pertofrane) and bupropion (Wellbutrin) that have little or no effect on serotonin are also effective antidepressants. The future is quite bright in terms of research that will reveal more and more about the causes of depression. This knowledge should guide development of new antidepressants that have both greater effectiveness and fewer side effects.

How can I deal with the dry mouth caused by some antidepressants? Dry mouth is a common side effect of tricyclic antidepressant medications. Usually, this symptom is mild and tolerable and requires no treatment. If it becomes troublesome, however, a variety of measures may be helpful. They include taking sips of water, sucking on sugarless hard candy (such as lemon drops), or chewing gum. Candies and gums that contain sugar should be avoided, and good oral hygiene (regular brushing and flossing) should be practiced. If dryness is especially severe, your doctor may prescribe a saliva substitute (Orex, Xero-Lube, Moi-Stir, Salivant, VA Oralube, and others), a saliva-stimulating medication (pilocarpine), or switch you to a different antidepressant.

What can I do if an antidepressant drug causes constipation? Constipation may be associated with depression itself and may actually disappear as the antidepressant drug begins to work. On the other hand, constipation may also be a side effect of antidepressants (especially tricyclics; see Table 1) and, while generally mild, may occasionally be troublesome. Preventive measures are usually quite effective. These include proper attention to diet, being sure to include fruit and vegetables and other sources of bulk such as bran as well as an adequate fluid intake. Regular meals, sleep, and exercise are also important. Excessive concern about having a daily bowel movement should be discouraged as should the regular use of laxatives, suppositories, and enemas.

Should constipation not be responsive to the above measures, your doctor may suggest the use of a stool softener such as docusate (Colace, DDS, Dialose, Regutol, Surfax, and others) or a bulk laxative such as psyllium hydrophyllic mucilloid (Correctol, Effer-Syllium, Fiberall, Hydrocil, Metamucil, and others).

Finally, since the antidepressants vary considerably in their tendency to cause constipation, switching to a less constipating drug may be helpful.

What can I do about the lightheaded feelings I get when I stand up? Lightheadedness or dizziness occurring on arising from lying down or sitting is usually due to a temporary fall in blood pressure, which can be caused or aggravated by some of the antidepressant drugs. If severe, this may result in loss of consciousness (blacking out), falls, and, sometimes, injuries. Usually such symptoms, if they occur at all, are mild and can be prevented or relieved by getting up slowly—sitting for several seconds before standing rather than standing up quickly. It is also important to avoid becoming dehydrated (dried out) since this can make lightheadedness worse. Thus, proper attention to drinking adequate fluids is necessary. Finally, if symptoms persist (they usually improve over time) or if they are severe, contact your doctor since it may be necessary to adjust your medication or use other corrective measures. Switching to a different antidepressant may be beneficial since not all drugs cause this problem.

What can I do if I feel sleepy? Sleepiness may diminish as your body grows accustomed to the antidepressant. Your doctor may suggest taking the majority or all of the medication in the evening so that most of the sedative effect will occur while you are asleep. Morning "hangover" can often be decreased by taking the medication shortly after dinner rather than at bedtime. If drowsiness is a persistent problem, your doctor can switch you to another antidepressant with less sedative effects. Caution should be exercised with regard to driving or operating machinery until sedative side effects have been resolved.

What can I do if I feel restless, nervous, or agitated? These symptoms can be caused by antidepressants although they may also be part of the underlying depression. If they are drug-induced they may improve over time but if treatment is necessary dosage reduction, the short-term use of an antianxiety drug, or switching to a different antidepressant will help. Be sure that caffeine in your diet is not adding to the problem.

If I do switch medicines because of side effects, do I have to stop one before I can start another? The answer is no if you are switching between the cyclic antidepressants found in Table 1. However, different doctors make the switch in different ways. Some stop one medicine, then begin the second right away or after a brief interval without medication. Others decrease the dose of the first drug while increasing the dose of the second drug.

Lithium can be added to cyclic and MAOI antidepressants, so no problem should arise if you are switched to lithium.

If you are changing from a cyclic antidepressant to an MAOI or vice versa, or from one MAOI to another, you may need to stop the first drug for at least 2 weeks before starting the second. (Fluoxetine [Prozac] must be stopped for at least 5 weeks before starting an MAOI.) There are some exceptions to this rule, but patients should never make this decision on their own because very serious elevations in blood pressure or other severe reactions can result from improper combinations of cyclic antidepressants and MAOIs.

Will antidepressants cause me to gain weight? Depression causes many people to lose weight by taking away appetite and interest in food. When depression lessens, good appetite returns and the lost weight may be regained. Unwanted weight gain is sometimes a side effect of antidepressant drugs because they may stimulate appetite, cause cravings for sweets, or alter how calories are processed and stored in the body. Unwanted weight gain may cause a person to stop taking an antidepressant even though the risk of getting depressed again is quite high. The side effect of weight gain is common with most tricyclic antidepressants, MAOIs, and lithium but is far less likely to occur with the newer antidepressants such as bupropion (Wellbutrin), fluoxetine (Prozac), sertraline (Zoloft), and trazodone (Desyrel).

Are the newer antidepressants better than the older ones? Overall, the percentage of depressed people responding to the newer drugs (such as bupropion [Wellbutrin], fluoxetine [Prozac], and sertraline [Zoloft]) is no better or worse than that for older drugs such as tricyclics and MAOIs. Whether certain types of depression respond better to one drug than another has not been fully resolved. What is clear is that the newer antidepressants differ substantially from the older ones in terms of side effect profiles and, on the whole, are better tolerated. They are less likely to cause sedation, dry mouth, blurred vision, constipation, weight gain, and heart problems. On the other hand, they are not without side effects and are more likely to cause nervousness, insomnia, headaches, and nausea. Selecting the proper drug for a given person is part of the art and science of medicine—there is no single drug that is best for everyone.

What's the difference between the generic and trade names of drugs? Generic names are the names given to chemical compounds. Trade names are used by drug companies to identify their particular brand of a generic drug. For example, in soft drinks, cola is the generic name, whereas Coke and Pepsi are trade names. Generic name drugs are often less expensive than trade-name drugs. Although equivalent doses of generic drugs contain the same amount of antidepressant, they may differ in bioavailability (the amount of drug getting into the body and reaching the sites of action in the brain). Because of possible differences in bioavailability, it may be best to continue with a single brand throughout a course of treatment. Some doctors feel that there is enough variability among different generic preparations of the same drug that they prefer to stick to trade-names. The newer antidepressants are protected by patent and are available only as the trade-name preparation. Once the patent expires other companies can market generic forms and prices often drop.

Do antidepressant medications make people suicidal? To the contrary, there is good evidence that by combating depression, antidepressants relieve suicidal thoughts and reduce risk of suicide. There have been some reports of people becoming suicidal or more suicidal during treatment. It is possible that a side effect of agitation may increase the level of distress in a depressed individual, and it is possible that relief from the immobility of depression may allow a person to act on suicidal thoughts before the depression fully lifts.

It is vitally important that these unlikely possibilities be placed in proper perspective. The risk of suicide from the treatment of depression is minuscule compared with the risk of suicide from untreated depression. During treatment the possibility of suicide should be assessed frequently until the person has fully recovered.

Monoamine Oxidase
Inhibitor Antidepressants

MAOIs are thought to exert their antidepressant effect by slowing the breakdown of neurotransmitters that may be reduced in amount in people with depression. This explanation is an oversimplification, but it provides a rationale for the use of these medications, which have been shown to be effective antidepressants.

There are three MAOI antidepressants currently available

TABLE 2. Monoamine oxidase inhibitor antidepressants

Generic name	Trade name	Usual starting dose	Usual therapeutic daily dose
isocarboxazid	Marplan	10 mg twice daily	30–40 mg
phenelzine	Nardil	15 mg twice daily	60–90 mg
tranylcypromine	Parnate	10 mg twice daily	30–60 mg

in the United States: isocarboxazid (Marplan), phenelzine (Nardil), and tranylcypromine (Parnate). Table 2 shows the usual starting and daily doses for adults.

In contrast to tricyclic antidepressants, which are often taken in a single dose at bedtime, MAOIs are usually taken in divided doses and avoided at bedtime. This is because many persons find these drugs to be activating, and insomnia can be a side effect.

Other MAOI side effects include restlessness, dizziness (including the type of dizziness caused by a drop in blood pressure when standing), and weight gain. Occasionally people experience extreme afternoon drowsiness as a side effect from these drugs.

There is one uncommon but potentially dangerous adverse reaction that is unique to MAOI antidepressants. These drugs inhibit the oxidase enzyme that breaks down ''monoamines'' at many places in the body, including the intestine. Consequently, people taking MAOIs may absorb more ''monoamine'' than usual. Certain foods contain large amounts of tyramine, a monoamine that affects blood pressure. Large amounts of tyramine may lead to extreme elevations in blood pressure (a hypertensive reaction), sometimes to the point of breaking blood vessels in the brain and causing a stroke or even death. Foods likely to cause this hypertensive reaction are listed in Table 3. Your doctor should provide you with a similar list. Although most medications are compatible with MAOIs, those that are not can be quite dangerous (see Table 3).

It is best for people taking MAOIs to avoid these foods and medications altogether, although some patients have used small amounts of some of these substances without experiencing a hypertensive reaction. However, the amount of potentially dangerous substances in foods can vary widely, so what seemed safe at one time may cause problems at another.

Although the list of foods and drugs to avoid may seem quite long and complicated, most people have no difficulty following the instructions. The likelihood of a serious reaction is quite small.

MAOIs are almost always a second-line treatment for depression. They are never indicated as the first antidepressant medication for typical depression. Some physicians might select them first for atypical depressions that are characterized by extreme fatigue, increased sleeping and/or appetite, and exaggerated fear of being rejected. Even then, a cyclic antidepressant is usually the first antidepressant used, with the MAOIs being kept in reserve. Some depressed people, however, respond only to MAOIs, and they should not be deprived of treatment because of dietary considerations.

Questions About MAOIs

How would I know if I were having a hypertensive reaction? Mild hypertensive reactions may go unnoticed.

TABLE 3. Substances that can cause a hypertensive reaction in patients taking an MAOI

Foods

Patients taking MAOIs must avoid these foods:

- Aged cheese in any form. Cottage and cream cheese are permitted.

- Yogurt

- Marmite, Bovril, and similar concentrated yeast or meat extracts (beware of drinks and stews made with these products). Baked products raised with yeast are allowed.

- Pickled herring

- Liver

- Alcohol in more than social (i.e., moderate) amounts. (Limit yourself to one glass of beer, wine, or sherry. Avoid Chianti wines altogether. You might take more if you are drinking only gin or vodka, but remember that one drink of alcohol may have a much greater effect when you are taking an MAOI.)

- Broad bean pods (limas, fava, Chinese, English, etc.) and banana skins

- Canned figs

- Food that is not fresh (or prepared from frozen or newly opened canned food). Take special care to avoid pickled, fermented, smoked, or aged meat, fish, poultry, game, or variety meats (organ meats and offal).

TABLE 3. Substances that can cause a hypertensive reaction in patients taking an MAOI (continued)

- Caffeine in large amounts (watch out for caffeine in cola drinks)
- Chocolate in large amounts
- Any food that has given unpleasant symptoms previously

Some patients discover that they can consume small quantities of "forbidden" foods without having a hypertensive reaction. Before making any deviations from these dietary restrictions, you should discuss them with your doctor.

Medicines

While most medications are compatible with MAOIs, those that are not can be quite dangerous. Some medications in combination with MAOIs may cause hypertensive or other severe reactions. Consequently, patients taking MAOIs should not take any medicines, drugs, over-the-counter preparations (including cough and cold preparations) or any other medication of any sort whatsoever without consulting their doctor. Make every doctor you see aware that you are taking an MAOI. Ordinary aspirin and acetaminophen (such as Tylenol) are all right if they are not part of a combination preparation for colds.

Marked elevation in blood pressure may be signaled by headache, stiff neck, pounding heartbeat, and, less frequently, nausea, vomiting, and dilated pupils.

What if I have a bad headache but no other symptoms? If the headache is of the kind and severity you often have (an "old friend"), you may decide to treat it with aspirin or acetaminophen (but not with combination cold remedies) and see how you feel. If the headache is atypical, unusually severe, or if your usual treatment is ineffective, you should contact your doctor or go to an emergency room for evaluation.

If I have a recognizable hypertensive reaction, what should I do? Go to your doctor's office or an emergency room immediately so your blood pressure can be measured. If it is elevated, appropriate treatment can be given.

Is there anything I can do about hypertensive reactions if I can't get to an emergency room? Some doctors give their patients on MAOI medication an antidote to carry in case a hypertensive reaction occurs. The most commonly recommended drug for this purpose is nifedipine (Procardia, Adalat). It is safer and more effective than chlorpromazine (Thorazine), which had been used occasionally in the past. Should a reaction occur and help not be readily available, a dose or two may be beneficial. However, it's best to actually measure blood pressure before starting treatment, and it's best that such treatment be done under close observation by a physician. If you suspect a hypertensive reaction, you should certainly stop taking your MAOI medication and see your doctor to determine whether or not your blood pressure has increased. Appropriate corrective steps can then be taken.

Lithium

Lithium is often effective in controlling manic-depressive disorder (also called bipolar mood disorder), which is characterized by wide and often disabling mood swings. In manic-depressive disorder, mood can be elevated—with feelings of elation, expansiveness, and euphoria—or depressed (see page 10). Lithium tends to stabilize mood at a more normal level. In this condition, lithium is beneficial in ending manic and depressive episodes as well as preventing their recurrence.

Lithium may be an effective antidepressant for some people who have only depression without ever experiencing any manic episodes. It is also useful as a long-term treatment to prevent recurrences of depressive episodes.

However, lithium treatment is somewhat complicated (although not particularly dangerous) and many nonpsychiatric physicians have not been trained in its use. If your doctor prescribes lithium as a treatment for your depression, you should read *Lithium and Manic Depression: A Guide* (see Suggested Readings).

Combinations of Antidepressants and Other Medications Used in the Treatment of Depression

Combinations of various cyclic antidepressants or a few cyclic and MAOI antidepressants are sometimes effective when single drugs have failed to help a patient. Although combining antidepressants can be quite beneficial, certain combinations can be dangerous. Consequently, these treatment approaches are usually left to specialists.

Adding lithium to a cyclic or MAOI antidepressant is often

effective in overcoming an otherwise resistant depression. This combination is usually straightforward, and many physicians have learned to use it effectively and with the precautions necessary to minimize risks.

Other medications are sometimes prescribed at the same time as antidepressants in an attempt to increase their effectiveness. These additional medications would not ordinarily be used if a satisfactory response is obtained with a cyclic antidepressant, an MAOI, or lithium alone. Among the medications shown to have some beneficial additive effect are thyroid hormone, L-tryptophan (an amino acid that is a building block for one neurotransmitter—it was recently withdrawn from the market in the United States because of toxic impurities found in some preparations), buspirone (BuSpar), and, occasionally, stimulants such as dextroamphetamine (Dexedrine) or methylphenidate (Ritalin).

Questions About
Other Medications

Why would other medications be helpful in some cases and not in others? There are many causes of depression. Each of these other medications may treat a different aspect of the several probable causes of depression. Thus, *thyroid hormone* may deal with one aspect of a hormonal imbalance that may accompany severe depression. The goal in using L-tryptophan is to increase the amount of available neurotransmitter by a different mechanism than the one involved in the use of cyclic antidepressants or MAOIs. The role of *stimulants* is controversial, in part because they have a clear potential for abuse, but, nevertheless, they seem helpful for some patients when carefully used for short periods of time. Two anticonvulsant drugs, *carbamazepine (Tegretol)* and *valproate (Depakote)* are being used experimentally, both alone and in combination with antidepressants or lithium, to treat some resistant forms of depression and manic-depression. Guides to the use of carbamazepine and valproate in bipolar disorder are listed in the Suggested Readings section (page 103).

Why not use a combination of medications all the time? Every medication has side effects and when more than one is used, it is likely that more side effects will occur. Also, certain combinations are potentially dangerous (combinations of MAOIs and stimulants or certain cyclic antidepressants, for example). Finally, cyclic antidepressants, MAOIs, or lithium alone are usually effective in treating depression so that combinations, with the added complications they may produce, are often unnecessary.

What about combination drugs such as Limbitrol, Triavil, and Etrafon? Limbitrol is a combination of the tricyclic antidepressant amitriptyline and a minor tranquilizer or antianxiety drug, chlordiazepoxide. Triavil and Etrafon combine amitriptyline and perphenazine, a major tranquilizer or antipsychotic drug. The idea behind these combinations is to provide some relief from anxiety, a prominent part of many depressions, with chlordiazepoxide or perphenazine while awaiting the antidepressant effect of the amitriptyline.

Proponents claim that these combinations permit a lower overall dose of amitriptyline and speedier symptomatic relief. Opponents point out that amitriptyline alone is as effective in the long run, that chlordiazepoxide has a potential for producing dependency, and perphenazine, although not causing dependency, can cause a disturbing disorder of abnormal movements called tardive dyskinesia. Any drug combination is inherently more complicated to use than a single medication. Finally, amitriptyline, which is one of the more sedating tricyclic antidepressants, when combined with chlordiazepoxide or perphenazine, which also have some sedating properties, may prove too sedating for some patients.

There is one type of depression, psychotic depression, for which the combination of an antidepressant and antipsychotic drug is more effective than an antidepressant alone.

What about alprazolam (Xanax) as an antidepressant? Alprazolam is an antianxiety drug or minor tranquilizer of the benzodiazepine family. Other drugs in the same class include chlordiazepoxide (Librium), clorazepate (Tranxene), diazepam (Valium), lorazepam (Ativan), oxazepam (Serax), and prazepam (Centrax).

Some, but not all, studies have shown alprazolam to have antidepressant properties as well as the antianxiety and antipanic effect for which it is currently indicated and prescribed. The dose of alprazolam required for antidepressant benefit may be higher than the effective antianxiety dose. This would tend to increase the likelihood of drowsiness, the main side effect of alprazolam. There is also a risk of developing physical dependence on the benzodiazepine drugs, especially when taken for long periods and in large doses as might be needed for the treatment of depression. On the other hand, alprazolam is free from certain side effects (especially cardiac and anticholinergic) that can be troublesome when tricyclic antidepressants are used.

At present, the use of alprazolam (Xanax) for depression remains experimental and it is not approved by the Food and Drug Administration (FDA) for this indication. Most doctors will not routinely use alprazolam for depression unless further research better defines its strengths and limitations.

Electroconvulsive Therapy (ECT)

In the experience and judgment of many physicians (and patients with severe depressions who have received ECT and other antidepressant treatments), electroconvulsive or "shock" therapy is the single most effective treatment for severe depression and has a number of advantages over other treatments.

ECT works rapidly so that patients can quickly return to productive living. It has a higher success rate for severe depression than any other single treatment approach.

ECT is the treatment of choice when a depressed person is making dangerous suicide attempts, because attempts are exceedingly rare after a course of treatment has been started.

In psychotic depression where a person has lost contact with reality and has delusions and/or hallucinations (see page 2), ECT is more effective than most antidepressant medications (an exception may be amoxapine [Asendin], which has been shown to be useful for psychotic depression).

Depressed patients who are also severely medically ill usually tolerate ECT very well and with fewer complications than when treated with antidepressant drugs. Contrary to the common fears and dramatic misconceptions often associated with the terms "shock treatment" and "electroconvulsive therapy," the actual physiological stress and risk from the minimal electrical stimulus employed are very low. In the most severe cases of depression, ECT can be lifesaving. For example, an 84-year-old woman with diabetes and heart failure was also severely depressed and highly agitated (physically overactive) because of her depression. The agitation aggravated the heart failure and her life was in great jeopardy for this reason. Though in very poor physical condition, she tolerated and responded promptly to three electroconvulsive treatments on successive days. Relieved of her depression and constant agitation, she became cooperative with her cardiac and diabetic treatments and progressed to recovery.

ECT is administered *after* the patient is put to sleep with a short-acting anesthetic and *after* the patient's muscles are relaxed so that muscle contractions from the treatment will not damage muscles or bones. Patients do not remember or feel the treatment.

After most treatments, there is a brief period of confusion and memory loss for recent events. This usually lasts from 20 to 60 minutes. *Temporary* memory loss increases with the number and frequency of treatments but can be lessened by increasing the interval between treatments and by "unilateral" or one-sided treatment. A new technique called brief-pulse ECT uses the minimum amount of electricity needed to produce an effective treatment and substantially reduces memory loss after each treatment and over a course of treatments.

Contrary to scare stories and subjective reports of lasting memory loss, repeated neuropsychological studies have failed to find any permanent effect on memory. In fact, memory is sometimes improved after ECT, probably because depression itself can have an adverse effect on memory. After the usual series of 6 to 12 treatments at intervals of 2 to 3 days, some decreasing memory loss may persist for as long as several months. Occasionally, patients complain of more persistent memory impairment, which may not be apparent when tested objectively. Whether this is a reflection of insensitive testing procedures and whether this is truly a consequence of ECT continues to be investigated. Once patients are given information about the great effectiveness and safety of ECT, they may prefer ECT to alternative treatments.

A guide to understanding ECT is available and can be found in the Suggested Readings section that begins on page 103.

New and
Less Frequently
Used Treatments

Exercise

Research over the past 15 years has shown that exercise has an antidepressant effect for many patients with mild to moderate depression. Exercise has not been shown to be of benefit in severe depression. No one is certain how exercise exerts its mood-elevating effect. Some experts believe that simply moving large muscle masses in regular rhythmical ways is inconsistent with depression. Others maintain that exercise produces a fundamental alteration in brain chemistry, perhaps affecting neurotransmitters and endorphins (recently discovered, naturally occurring morphine-like substances).

To be effective against depression, exercise must be done regularly at least three times and preferably five or more times per week for sessions lasting at least half an hour. In order to be able to carry on such an active program of exercise, the exercise must be comfortable, and it is here that problems often arise. Many people starting to exercise have in their mind's eye an image of the world's best athletes. This may lead them to push too hard, become sore, fatigued, and possibly even injured. As a result, they understandably quit exercise before they have had a chance to obtain the benefits exercise can provide. Older individuals and those with medical problems should consult with their physician before beginning an exercise program.

A combination of walking and running is the single most common form of exercise used for the treatment of depression. However, any regular aerobic exercise (done without building an oxygen debt—a simple test of aerobic exercise is the ability to whistle or carry on a conversation *while* exercising) program is likely to provide comparable benefits. Walking/running is the most practical approach to exercise for most people because it is inexpensive, requires no equipment beyond comfortable clothes and a good pair of shoes, is possible in all weather, and can be done alone or with others. Swimming, bicycling, rowing, and aerobic dance all have their advocates and devotees, but each requires facilities, equipment, or companions. Guides to using exercise for treating depression are found in Suggested Readings on page 103.

Phototherapy (Light Therapy)

Some people have seasonal depressions that recur regularly in the winter and appear to be associated with a reduction in daylight hours (seasonal affective disorder, or SAD). These depressions fade away as spring approaches and may be followed by a period of mild hyperactivity. There is considerable support for exposure to *bright* light being an effective treatment for winter depressions. Individuals usually sit about 3 feet away from 6 to 8 fluorescent bulbs—ordinary room light is too dim to be effective. After several days of exposure (usually on arising for ½ to 2 hours daily), the depression improves and remains improved as long as treatment continues. Although this approach is still under investigation, many clinicians are recommending it for this particular type of depression. Treatment should be under the supervision of a professional who is experienced with SAD and its treatment.

Sleep Deprivation

Recent studies have begun to confirm earlier case reports that some individuals with severe depression are transiently helped by remaining awake all night. A few individuals have been treated with this approach alone and are able to maintain a recovery from depression by continued judicious use of sleep deprivation. Others gain temporary relief from sleep deprivation alone but require antidepressant medications to maintain their gains. However, some do not benefit at all.

The mechanism by which sleep deprivation alleviates depression is unclear. Some researchers think that most depressed people have a phase shift in their basic circadian or 24-hour rhythms and that sleep deprivation helps correct this abnormality.

At this time, sleep deprivation is an experimental treatment and should not be used to the exclusion of other treatments that have been proven to be effective. Patients should not treat themselves with this experimental approach, and only clinicians who are experienced in the use and effects of sleep deprivation should offer this treatment.

Psychosurgery

In very rare cases of depression where all other treatments have failed, careful neurosurgical interruption of brain pathways has been shown to help about 50% of patients. The neurosurgical procedures are done under the control of exact three-dimensional measurements (stereotactic) so that the interruption of brain pathways is precisely defined and limited. The techniques are surprisingly safe and seldom cause complications in the form of personality change or epilepsy. Death as a result of this surgery is rare.

Although clearly not to be undertaken lightly, psychosurgery has a place in the treatment of the most difficult cases of depression. We would never recommend psychosurgery until and unless all other treatments had been given a full trial and found to be ineffective. In our hands, psychosurgery would never be recommended until 2 years had passed, during which the full spectrum of alternative treatments had been tried and a spontaneous remission had failed to appear. Even then, we would recommend psychosurgery only for patients with severe depression that is causing them extreme distress or disability.

Some Common Questions About the Treatment of Depression

W ho is the best professional to treat depression? Because primary care doctors (family or general practitioners or internists), psychiatrists (who are also physicians), and psychologists all treat depression, this is a common question and an understandable source of confusion.

Because most individuals with depressions requiring treatment should be evaluated medically, and because antidepressant drug therapy is often indicated, a physician is the obvious first choice when seeking professional help. Your primary care doctor already knows a great deal about your medical history, your family, and other important aspects of your life. He or she is an appropriate person to evaluate your depression and begin treatment if it is necessary. In most cases, this first treatment will be effective. If depression persists, your doctor knows the other doctors (psychiatrists or psychologists) who specialize in treating depression and will be able to make the most appropriate referral.

So, unless special circumstances exist (such as a suicide attempt, a depression of psychotic magnitude, a depression in a patient with manic-depressive disorder, or prior treatment by a depression specialist), it is quite reasonable that depression first be evaluated and treated by the primary care doctor who will arrange referral if necessary.

Which treatment is best for depression?   Because depression is almost certainly caused by different factors, there is no single best treatment for depression. The best treatment for any individual's depression is the treatment that counteracts the causes of that particular depression. However, it is often impossible to pinpoint the causes of depression, so treatment is often begun on the basis of what is most often helpful for most depressions. Frequently this means antidepressant medications.

Am I to blame for being depressed?   It is unfortunate that so many depressed people hold themselves responsible for their depressions. All too commonly, others reinforce this misconception by mistaking depression as an indication only of weak will. Not only are these perspectives incorrect, they are also demoralizing. It is the depression, itself, that distorts a patient's normal way of thinking and leads to symptoms of self-blame and guilt. Remember that depression is a medical disorder and that blaming yourself or another for being depressed would be like blaming yourself or them for developing arthritis or high blood pressure. The false belief shared by far too many people that depressed individuals bring it all on themselves and could feel better merely by trying harder could not be further from the truth. Depression is a painful, unpleasant illness that a sufferer would not wish on him- or herself or anyone else.

Is taking antidepressants a sign of weakness? *NO!* Depression is a medical disorder, just as diabetes and pneumonia are medical disorders. People with depression need treatment, and antidepressant medicines are just as important in the treatment of depression as insulin is in the treatment of diabetes and antibiotics are for pneumonia.

If you are only working too hard or are unhappy because of a life situation that would make anyone unhappy, will antidepressant medication be useful? Generally not. At times, however, it is difficult to distinguish between ordinary "blues" or discouragement and the illness of depression. Sometimes it is an underlying depression that causes difficult life situations rather than the other way around. When in doubt, evaluation by a professional is appropriate.

Which antidepressant am I likely to receive? If you have a common form of depression, then one of the cyclic antidepressants listed in Table 1 on page 57 will probably be prescribed, since they are currently the standard treatment for depression.

What if the first treatment doesn't work? Unfortunately, even the treatments that are usually effective may not help a given individual. Fortunately, alternative treatments are likely to be helpful, and it is important to keep working with your doctor until an effective treatment is found. If several treatments have not improved your condition, you and your doctor may benefit from a second opinion or consultation with another clinician.

Can I stop the antidepressant medicines as soon as I feel better? *NO!* It appears that antidepressants merely alleviate the symptoms of depression until the depression runs its course. Because depressions often last from a few months to many years if untreated, you would be likely to experience a relapse if you stop your antidepressant medicine too soon. You and your doctor should work together to decide when it would be appropriate to decrease and then discontinue your medication.

What happens if I forget to take my antidepressant medicine? If you are taking several doses each day and forget one, do not add it to the next dose unless instructed to do so by your doctor. Merely continue with the recommended dosing schedule. If you take all of your medication in the evening, do not try to make up the missed dose the next morning, but simply make certain that you take the correct dose the following evening and on subsequent evenings. If you are taking a single dose in the morning and forget, take it later in the day unless it is too close to bedtime and may interfere with sleep. Doubling your dose in a single day might cause annoying or dangerous side effects.

It is important to take antidepressant medications as prescribed; that means taking all of the medication at the correct time(s). Missing a single dose is unlikely to cause problems, but missing doses repeatedly could cause a return of depression.

How long do I have to take antidepressant medicine? The length of treatment varies among individuals. It is determined by the frequency of depressive episodes and by how effective and tolerable the antidepressant treatment is for each person. Although continuous antidepressant treatment is helpful in certain cases, many people will not require it. The usual course of treatment runs from 4 months to 1 year. The best course of treatment for each person must be developed individually with the doctor. If a drug is not working after 4 to 6 weeks at an adequate dose, continued treatment is rarely indicated and an alternative drug should be used. For individuals who have had previous depressive episodes, long-term (indefinite) treatment may be indicated to prevent further episodes.

What about antidepressant drugs and pregnancy? Ideally, all medications should be avoided when a woman is trying to become pregnant and during at least the first 3 months of pregnancy. This approach will minimize the likelihood of a malformed baby. In some cases, however, a medication may be so necessary to a woman's health that it cannot be discontinued. Fortunately, there is no good evidence that the cyclic or monoamine oxidase inhibitor (MAOI) antidepressants are associated with a higher than normal risk of malformations (lithium, carbamazepine, and valproate are somewhat riskier), and most women have had normal pregnancies and deliveries despite taking these drugs throughout pregnancy. Because individual circumstances vary, a prospective mother taking antidepressants should discuss her medication with her doctor before she decides to become pregnant.

There are no known harmful effects from antidepressants on children whose fathers were taking antidepressants at the time of conception or whose mothers were taking antidepressants prior to but not during conception. Remember that it may take several days or weeks for an antidepressant to completely leave the body once it is discontinued.

Antidepressant drugs are excreted in breast milk, and although the concentrations are quite low, a decision to breastfeed should be made in consultation with the doctor.

Do children and adolescents get depressed? Unfortunately, the answer is yes. Depression is much more common in children and adolescents than once believed. For reasons that are not well understood, there has been a trend toward an earlier age at onset of depression (and manic-depression) in people born since the 1940s. Also, clinicians are doing a better job of looking for and recognizing depression in these age groups. Quite often, depression in young people consists of the same symptoms as found in adults. At times, however, the diagnosis may be more elusive. The youngsters may not recognize the discomfort that they are experiencing is an illness known as depression.

Although young children may not be able to express their sad mood in words, they often show it with persistent sad expressions. Other indications of depression are loss of motivation and enthusiasm, fatigue, difficulty making decisions, social withdrawal, weight change (up or down), irritability and anger, deterioration of school performance, truancy, acting out and behavioral difficulties, and physical complaints.

Families or teachers may recognize behavioral changes indicative of depression even though the youngster may deny being depressed. Whenever depression is suspected, the child should be evaluated by a doctor experienced in working with this age group. Just as in adults, depression in young people can have a number of causes, and recognizing these causes can lead to very effective treatments. Recognizing and treating depression in youngsters is especially important considering the critical stages of development they are passing through. Also, there has been a disturbing increase in suicide in adolescents over the last few decades, and although suicide is quite rare in children, it does occur. Treatments for childhood and adolescent depression are the same as those used in adults and include psychotherapies and medications and combinations thereof.

Do depressed children need medicines?   Many doctors remain cautious about prescribing medications for children who are still growing and developing. Although antidepressants appear to be safe for children, concern remains about the possibility of unknown negative effects on their growth and development. On the other hand, depression itself can have devastating effects on a child's emotional and intellectual growth and development and can lead to suicide, even in young children. Antidepressant medications are effective in treating depression in many children and may be lifesaving, but the use of these medications requires full consideration of the possible risks and benefits.

Can older people take antidepressant medication?   Depression in the elderly can be severe, debilitating, and deadly. Fortunately, advanced age is no barrier to the successful treatment of depression. Because the elderly are likely to have associated medical illnesses, may be taking other medications, and are more sensitive to drug side effects, the use of antidepressant drugs can be more complicated than in younger persons. In general, antidepressants are less well tolerated and the possibility of adverse drug interactions is greater in the elderly. Consequently, close collaboration between treating physician and consultants is essential. The side effect profiles of some antidepressants make them better suited for use in the elderly. In brief, antidepressant drugs can be used both effectively and safely in the elderly.

How will I feel while taking antidepressant medications? The main effect of antidepressants is to *lift or elevate mood* from a depressed level to a normal one. Once mood is returned to normal, antidepressants *stabilize* mood and usually prevent a return of depression as long as they are taken. Some side effects are likely to occur. Side effects such as decreased worry or anxiety and increased sleep are quite welcome. Other side effects, although annoying, are usually tolerable and often lessen as time passes. Occasionally, side effects are problematic to the point that changing to a different drug is necessary.

What if I am on a special diet? Most antidepressants can be used without problems regardless of a person's diet. Monoamine oxidase inhibitors (MAOIs) are exceptions and require certain dietary precautions to avoid dangerous interactions (see Table 3 on pages 70–71). High dietary caffeine intake may worsen side effects of anxiety, nervousness, and insomnia that are caused by some antidepressants. Alcohol can interact adversely with antidepressants and many clinicians discourage its use during treatment with antidepressant drugs. Alcohol does *not* increase the effectiveness of antidepressants and may actually interfere with their action.

Diets that restrict salt or fluid intake may increase the risk of lithium toxicity. Consequently, individuals taking lithium should discuss proposed diet changes with their doctor.

What about vitamins and minerals? There is no sound evidence that vitamin or mineral supplements are useful in the treatment of depression. However, if a person chooses to take vitamin or mineral products as diet supplements, no adverse interactions with antidepressant medications would be expected. Infrequently, vitamin B_6 (pyridoxine) deficiency may be a factor in causing depression, usually in women taking oral contraceptives. In this case, supplementation of vitamin B_6 intake is important. Occasionally, other vitamin deficiencies can be associated with depression, as in vitamin B_{12} deficiency, which can cause pernicious anemia.

Can I exercise while on antidepressant drug treatment? *CERTAINLY!* Exercise is an important factor in everyone's health and has been shown to have antidepressant properties. Be sure to take in enough fluids and a normal amount of dietary salt. Salt pills are never needed.

Is it dangerous to take other medications while on antidepressant medicines? Although most medications can be safely combined with antidepressants, some may interact to cause serious side affects. It is important to tell all doctors treating you that you are taking an antidepressant medication. Before taking any medication (prescription or nonprescription), ask your doctor or pharmacist whether it might interact adversely with your antidepressant.

What about blood levels of antidepressant medications? Blood levels of many antidepressant drugs can now be accurately measured and these measurements sometimes prove helpful in adjusting drug doses. However, it is quite acceptable not to routinely measure antidepressant blood levels. With most antidepressants there is not a close correlation between blood level and clinical response. Blood levels of MAOIs are rarely obtained because direct assays are difficult to perform. Sometimes the extent to which an MAOI inhibits the enzyme monoamine oxidase is measured.

By contrast, determination of blood (serum) lithium levels is a simple, reliable laboratory procedure, essential to the proper management of lithium treatment.

Lithium levels are obtained frequently when starting treatment and after any change in dose. *It is very important that blood levels be determined in the morning, as near as possible to 12 hours after the evening dose and before the morning dose.*

Blood levels of antidepressants may be obtained to assist the physician in assessing how a given individual absorbs, metabolizes, and excretes the drug. There is up to a 30-fold difference in blood level with a given dose of antidepressant in different individuals. The usual clinical approach with most antidepressants is to increase the dose until depression is relieved, side effects become too severe, or a recommended upper limit is reached. Sometimes a low dose of drug will produce a very high blood level, and sometimes a very high dose will be associated with a very low blood level. Measuring the blood level is the only way to know if this has happened. A few medications seem to have a "therapeutic window" of effective blood level. The likelihood of an antidepressant response is greatly reduced at blood levels both below and above the "therapeutic window."

What if I need to see another doctor or have an operation while taking an antidepressant medication? When seeing other doctors or undergoing any medical, dental, or surgical procedure, always tell those involved that you are taking an antidepressant medication. This information should help ensure that your antidepressant medication is managed safely and effectively. Don't assume that being on an antidepressant is only important to the doctor who prescribes it for you.

Are antidepressant medicines the best treatment for depression? For many people, yes. However, not everyone can tolerate antidepressant medications, and not everyone is helped by them. Alternative treatment—psychotherapy, electroconvulsive therapy, exercise, light therapy (ECT), sleep deprivation, and, rarely, psychosurgery—is available to help those who do not benefit from antidepressant medications. Despite their limitations, antidepressant medications have been of benefit to millions of people. Only you and your doctor can determine whether antidepressant medications will be the best treatment for you.

Does it have to be either psychotherapy or medications? *NO!* All depressed patients need and can benefit from psychotherapy. But some patients with mild depression, most patients with moderate depression, and almost all patients with severe depression need medications as well as psychotherapy for best results. Overall, medications are more effective than psychotherapy, particularly when depression is severe. And when depression is most severe, patients can seldom benefit from psychotherapy alone.

For moderate depression, recent studies have shown that a combination of antidepressant medications and psychotherapy is more helpful for patients than either treatment alone (see page 52).

Even though it is hard to show any direct benefit of psychotherapy in severe depression and the effects of psychotherapy may be weaker than medications in less severe depression, psychotherapy does offer the understanding and support we all need in difficult times. It also provides the physician with an opportunity to monitor the patient's response to treatment with antidepressant medications.

After the worst of a depression is over, psychotherapy may be helpful in identifying factors that have led to depression and may help a person make changes that can reduce the likelihood of subsequent depressions. It is also quite helpful in dealing with psychological and social problems caused by the depression.

Are antidepressant medications addictive? *NO!* They are not "dope," and if you stopped taking them, you would not have a craving for them. However, as with any medication that affects the central nervous system, it is wise to taper off the medication gradually so that your body has time to adjust to the change.

If these antidepressant medications improve my mood, aren't they like "pep pills" or "uppers" that people buy on the streets? *ABSOLUTELY NOT!* "Pep pills" or "uppers" give people a sudden burst of energy and distort their sense of reality, whether they are depressed or not. Pep pills and uppers can be dangerous and addicting. They are used to treat depression with close supervision only on rare occasions, and then usually for short periods of time. Antidepressant medicines do not improve *a nondepressed person's* mood, and the only effects a normal person is likely to experience are unwanted side effects such as dry mouth or sleepiness.

How safe are antidepressant medicines? Antidepressants are very safe when used as directed. Nevertheless, any medication can cause problems and you will want to follow your doctor's instructions closely to minimize the possibility of difficulties. Excessive amounts of antidepressants (overdoses) can be quite dangerous and sometimes deadly. Overdoses of some antidepressants are tolerated much better than others.

How bad are side effects from antidepressant medications? Most people notice few side effects and find the ones they do experience quite tolerable. Some patients have annoying side effects that make them "feel worse before they feel better." These side effects often decrease in severity as the body adjusts to the medication. A few people have such severe side effects that they cannot take a particular medication at all. Switching to a different antidepressant is often all that is necessary in these situations.

Overall, most people notice some side effects but can continue the medication and benefit from its antidepressant effect.

What if side effects from medications are severe? Most side effects are most troublesome at the beginning of treatment and then diminish in severity. If side effects are particularly severe, it is best not to take another dose of medication until you discuss the problem with your doctor. Sometimes simple adjustments in the dosage size or schedule will relieve intolerable side effects. Sometimes adding another medicine will relieve the side effect. At other times a change to another antidepressant may be helpful.

Will antidepressant medicines affect my sex life? Sex drive is often reduced in depression, and antidepressant medications, by treating depression, usually restore sex drive to a normal level. If sex drive has continued at a normal level in spite of depression, antidepressant medications usually have little effect on it. At times antidepressant medications can lower sex drive in both sexes and cause impotence or loss of orgasm in males and loss of orgasm in females. These problems are not permanent and can be relieved by reducing, stopping, or changing medication.

Do antidepressant medicines make people suicidal? Recently, the antidepressant fluoxetine (Prozac) has been in the news because of concerns that it may make people suicidal. Fortunately, there has been much more smoke than fire, and there is now good evidence that fluoxetine, like other antidepressants, actually makes depressed and suicidal individuals *less* depressed and *less* suicidal. It is important to realize that when being treated for depression, people often do not respond immediately, and some may get side effects from medications and actually feel worse. Consequently, suicide risk must be carefully assessed throughout the entire course of treatment.

It is certainly possible that a few people may actually become more suicidal while being treated with *any* antidepressant treatment, including antidepressant medications, psychotherapy, electroconvulsive therapy (ECT), light therapy, and exercise. If this is the case, such feelings should be shared with the doctor so that appropriate treatment modifications can be made. It is very apparent that not treating depression carries a far greater risk to far more people than do the side effects of antidepressant medications. To avoid treatment with fluoxetine or any other antidepressants because of ill-founded claims would be truly unfortunate.

Are there any late-appearing side effects of antidepressant medicines? Most people suffering from depression take antidepressant medicines for periods of a few months to a few years. However, antidepressant medications that have been used continuously for many years have not been found to produce late-appearing side effects. For example, there is absolutely no evidence that antidepressants cause or predispose an individual to cancer.

Lithium is something of a special case since it has been shown to cause underactivity of the thyroid gland (hypothyroidism) and reduction in kidney function in a few patients. Both of these conditions can be identified by routine laboratory tests and are usually corrected by simple measures.

Although long-term effects are either unknown or unrecognized (cyclic antidepressants and MAOIs) or easily identified so they can be dealt with before they become serious (lithium), physicians remain concerned about possible long-term side effects that might emerge very late in the course of treating depression with medications. Consequently, most physicians will talk with their patients about the relative risks of stopping medication (a new episode of depression might occur) versus the small or unknown risk of some late-developing side effect. Physicians also evaluate their patients periodically for new side effects that may be caused by continued use of medication.

Are antidepressant medications used for anything other than depression? Sometimes antidepressants are used for migraine headache or other kinds of pain that fail to respond to conventional treatments. Bed-wetting is sometimes treated with antidepressants. Panic disorder, some phobias, and obsessive-compulsive disorder are also treated with antidepressants, often in combination with behavioral psychotherapies. Although these conditions are often associated with depression, antidepressants are effective treatments even in the *absence* of depression. Just because a disorder is helped by an antidepressant does not automatically mean that a depression is present. Clomipramine (Anafranil) is both an antidepressant and an antiobsessive-compulsive drug. In the United States it is indicated only for the latter condition, and it works well even in the absence of depression.

How can someone learn all that is important about depression and its treatments? A book of this size cannot provide answers to every question that might be asked about depression. The material included here was selected because doctors and patients thought it was especially important.

The following suggestions may help you learn more about depression and the different ways of treating it:

- Read this book and be sure to note any areas where you have questions.
- Ask your doctor these questions and any others you might have.
- Reread this book from time to time to refresh your memory. Share it with close friends and family members and discuss areas that are particularly important to you.
- Refer to the readings suggested on the next few pages.
- There are self-help groups around the country that offer support and information to people with depression. The National Depressive and Manic-Depressive Association (NDMDA) can be contacted for information at:

NDMDA
730 North Franklin Street, Suite 501
Chicago, IL 60610
Tel (312) 642-0049
Fax (312) 642-7243

- Additional information can be obtained from the following resources:

D/ART Program (Depression/Awareness,
Recognition and Treatment)
National Institute of Mental Health
Room 15-C-05
5600 Fishers Lane
Rockville, MD 20857

and

The National Alliance for the Mentally Ill (NAMI)
2101 Wilson Boulevard, Suite 302
Arlington, VA 22201
Tel (703) 524-7600

- You can also contact the Information Centers at the University of Wisconsin Department of Psychiatry (see page 100) to find out if there is a self-help program in your area. There is no charge for this service.

Suggested
Readings

The following books may be helpful in better understanding depression, manic-depression, lithium, and mental illness:

Nontechnical

Andreasen NC: The Broken Brain: The Biological Revolution in Psychiatry. New York, Harper & Row, 1984

Bohn J, Jefferson JW: Lithium and Manic Depression: A Guide, Revised Edition. Madison, WI, Lithium Information Center, 1990

Burns DD: Feeling Good: The New Mood Therapy. New York, William Morrow and Company, 1980

DePaulo JR, Ablow KR: How to Cope With Depression: A

Complete Guide for You and Your Family. New York, McGraw-Hill, 1989

Eischens RR, Greist JH: Running Guides. Madison, WI, Center for Affective Disorders, 1984

Endler NS: Holiday of Darkness. New York, John Wiley & Sons, 1982

Fieve RR: Moodswing, Revised Edition. New York, William Morrow, 1989

Gold MS: The Good News About Depression. New York, Villard Books, 1987

Greist JH, Jefferson JW, Marks IM: Anxiety and Its Treatment: Help Is Available. Washington, DC, American Psychiatric Press, 1986 (also available as a Warner paperback)

Jefferson JW, Greist JH: Valproate and Manic Depression: A Guide. Madison, WI, Lithium Information Center, 1991

Kline NS: From Sad to Glad, Revised Edition. New York, Ballantine, 1987

Knauth P: A Season in Hell. New York, Harper & Row, 1975

Lewinsohn P, Munoz R, Youngren MA, et al: Control Your Depression. Englewood Cliffs, NJ, Prentice-Hall, 1979

Lobel B, Hirschfeld RMA: Depression: What We Know (DHHS Publ No ADM-85-1318). Rockville, MD, National Institute of Mental Health, 1985

Medenwald JR, Greist JH, Jefferson JW: Carbamazepine and Manic Depression: A Guide, Revised Edition. Madison, WI, Lithium Information Center, 1990

Miller MH: Psychiatry: A Personal View. New York, Scribner's, 1981

Morrison JR: Your Brother's Keeper: Confronting Psychiatric Illness. Chicago, IL, Nelson-Hall, 1981

Styron W: Darkness Visible: A Memoir of Madness. New York, Random House, 1990

Tsuang MT, VanderMey R: Genes and the Mind: Inheritance

of Mental Illness. New York, Oxford University Press, 1980

Wender PH, Klein DF: Mind, Mood, and Medicine. New York, Farrar Straus & Giroux/New American Library, 1981

Winokur G: Depression: The Facts. New York, Oxford University Press, 1981

Technical

American Psychiatric Association: Diagnostic and Statistical Manual of Mental Disorders, 3rd Edition, Revised. Washington, DC, American Psychiatric Association, 1987

Beck AT, Rush JT, Shaw B, et al: Cognitive Therapy of Depression. New York, Guilford, 1979

Goodwin FK, Jamison KR: Manic-Depressive Illness. New York, Oxford University Press, 1990

Greist JH, Greist TH: Antidepressant Treatment: The Essentials. Melbourne, FL, Krieger, 1979

Greist JH, Jefferson JW, Spitzer RL (eds): Treatment of Mental Disorders. New York, Oxford University Press, 1982

Jefferson JW, Greist JH, Ackerman DL, et al: Lithium Encyclopedia for Clinical Practice, 2nd Edition. Washington, DC, American Psychiatric Press, 1987

Klein DF, Gittelman R, Quitkin FV, et al: Diagnosis and Drug Treatment of Psychiatric Disorders: Adults and Children, Revised Edition. Baltimore, MD, Williams & Wilkins, 1980

Klerman GL, Weissman MM, Rounsaville BJ, et al: Interpersonal Psychotherapy of Depression. New York, Basic Books, 1984

Schatzberg AF, Cole JO: Manual of Clinical Psychopharmacology, 2nd Edition. Washington, DC, American Psychiatric Press, 1991

Strupp HH, Binder JL: Psychotherapy in a New Key: Time-Limited Dynamic Psychotherapy. New York, Basic Books, 1984

We hope to revise and update this book from time to time. Your comments, suggestions, and criticisms are most welcome. Please contact:

Information Centers
Department of Psychiatry
University of Wisconsin
Center for Health Sciences
600 Highland Avenue
Madison, WI 53792
Tel (608) 263-6171

Summing Up

Depression is a common disorder, and major depression affects at least 10% of the population at some point during their lifetime. Even larger percentages suffer from mild or moderate depression, and at any one point in time 5% of the population is experiencing depression severe enough to need treatment.

Depression can be very severe. People who have suffered both major depression and a serious medical illness such as a heart attack usually say that depression was by far the worse experience. Although medical problems are often confined to one organ system (such as the heart and blood vessels or "cardiovascular system"), depression has effects throughout the body and disrupts a person's feelings, thinking, behavior, and physical well-being. The most extreme behavioral abnormality caused by depression is suicide, which indicates the deep and pervasive pain depressed people can feel.

Although depression is usually easy to diagnose once it is considered, it is often unrecognized or confused with fatigue or frustration. It may be "masked" or hidden in physical complaints such as pain or psychological changes such as withdrawal, irritability, or anxiety. Unfortunately, many depressed people never seek or receive effective treatment—therefore many suffer and some die needlessly.

Depression tends to run in families and to reoccur. The causes of depression are currently unknown in most cases. Improper functioning of brain chemicals (neurotransmitters) is thought to be involved in all depressions. Occasionally, depression is caused by a medical illness (page 9) or alcohol, or even by prescription medications (page 21).

Recognition and diagnosis of depression are crucial first steps to recovery. Since many patients go to their general physician with complaints of fatigue, pain, irritability, or anxiety as well as frank depression, general physicians are in a good position to provide effective first-line diagnosis and treatment of depression. Psychiatrists, psychologists, and other mental health clinicians with special expertise and extensive experience in treating depression are often consulted by general physicians when routine treatments are ineffective. Some patients contact mental health clinicians directly for diagnosis and treatment of depression.

Antidepressant medications are the cornerstone of treatment for severe depression and also have an important role to play in the treatment of moderate and even mild depression. Most patients can take antidepressant medication safely and with only minimal side effects to achieve a rapid recovery from depression. The antidepressant medications stand in a class by themselves and are not sedatives, "downers," "uppers," or "dope." They are not addicting.

Psychotherapy is also used to treat depression. Present evidence indicates that a combination of antidepressant medication and psychotherapy is the best treatment for most depressions.

If basic treatments are ineffective, combinations of two or more medications or electroconvulsive therapy are often helpful.

Depression can have a devastating effect on patients and their families. Fortunately, helpful treatment is available, and most patients who receive treatment recover promptly and return to full functioning. The most difficult step to recovery from depression is the first one—recognizing that depression is a possibility and that recovery is highly likely if diagnosis and treatment are sought.

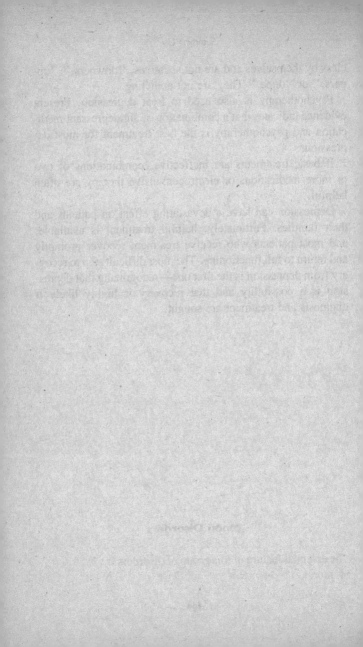

Appendix
DSM-III-R Mood Disorders

The material in this appendix has been excerpted from the *Diagnostic and Statistical Manual of Mental Disorders*, *Third Edition*, *Revised* (DSM-III-R), published in 1987 by the American Psychiatric Association, 1400 K Street, N.W., Washington, DC 20005.

Note: The page numbers referred to in the appendix that follows are the original page numbers that appear in DSM-III-R, and not page numbers from *Depression and Its Treatment*.

Mood Disorders

The essential feature of this group of disorders is a disturbance of mood, accompanied by a full or partial Manic or Depressive Syndrome, that is not due to any other physical or mental disorder. Mood refers to a prolonged emotion that colors the whole psychic life; it generally involves either depression or elation. In DSM-III this diagnostic class was called Affective Disorders.

The organization of the text for the Mood Disorders departs from the usual method of presentation in order to avoid redundancy, and includes the following:

Terminology used in the classification of Mood Disorders, p. 213
Subclassification of Mood Disorders, p. 214
Manic Episode, p. 214
Hypomanic Episode, p. 218
Major Depressive Episode, p. 218
   Chronic Type, p. 224
   Melancholia, p. 224
   Seasonal pattern, p. 224
BIPOLAR DISORDERS, p. 225
   Bipolar Disorder, p. 225
   Cyclothymia, p. 226
   Bipolar Disorder NOS, p. 228
DEPRESSIVE DISORDERS, p. 228
   Major Depression, p. 228
   Dysthymia, p. 230
   Depressive Disorder NOS, p. 233

Terminology used in classification of Mood Disorders. A *mood syndrome* (depressive or manic) is a group of mood and associated symptoms that occur together for a minimal duration of time. For example, the Major Depressive Syndrome is defined as depressed mood or loss of interest, of at least two weeks' duration, accompanied by several associated symptoms, such as weight loss and difficulty concentrating. Mood syndromes can occur as part of a Mood Disorder, as part of a nonmood psychotic disorder (e.g., Schizoaffective Disorder), or as part of an Organic Mental Disorder (e.g., Organic Mood Disorder).

A *mood episode* (major depressive, manic, or hypomanic) is a mood syndrome that is not due to a known organic factor and is not part of a nonmood psychotic disorder (e.g., Schizophrenia, Schizoaffective Disorder, or Delusional Disorder). For example, a Major Depressive Episode is a Major Depressive Syndrome (as defined above) in which it cannot be established that an organic factor initiated and maintained the disturbance and the presence of a nonmood psychotic disorder has been ruled out.

A *mood disorder* is determined by the pattern of mood episodes. For example, the diagnosis of Major Depression is made when there have been one or more Major Depressive Episodes without a history of a Manic or unequivocal Hypomanic Episode.

Subclassification of Mood Disorders. Mood Disorders are divided into Bipolar Disorders and Depressive Disorders. The essential feature of Bipolar Disorders is the presence of one or more Manic or Hypomanic Episodes (usually with a history of Major Depressive Episodes). The essential feature of Depressive Disorders is one or more periods of depression without a history of either Manic or Hypomanic Episodes.

There are two Bipolar Disorders: Bipolar Disorder, in which there is one or more Manic Episodes (usually with one or more Major Depressive Episodes); and Cyclothymia, in which there are numerous Hypomanic Episodes and numerous periods with depressive symptoms. Disorders with Hypomanic and full Major Depressive Episodes, sometimes referred to as "Bipolar II," are included in the residual category of Bipolar Disorder NOS.

There are two Depressive Disorders: Major Depression, in which there is one or more Major Depressive Episodes; and Dysthymia, in which there is a history of a depressed mood more days than not for at least two years and in which, during the first two years of the disturbance, the condition did not meet the criteria for a Major Depressive Episode. In many cases of Dysthymia, there are superimposed Major Depressions.

The current state of Major Depression or Bipolar Disorder is described with a fifth-digit code. If the criteria for a Major Depressive or Manic Episode are currently met, the episode is subclassified as either: mild, moderate, severe without psychotic features, or with psychotic features. If the criteria are currently not met, the fifth-digit code indicates whether the disorder is in partial or in full remission.

In addition, a current Major Depressive Episode can be specified as:

- *melancholic type*—a typically severe form of a Major Depressive Episode that is believed to be particularly responsive to somatic therapy (see p. 224 for criteria); or

- *chronic*—the current episode has lasted two consecutive years without a period of two months or longer in which there have been no depressive symptoms.

For Bipolar Disorder, Bipolar Disorder NOS, Recurrent Major Depression, and Depressive Disorder NOS, a further specification is:

- *seasonal pattern*—a regular cyclic relationship between

onset of the mood episodes and a particular 60-day period of the year (see p. 224 for criteria).

Manic Episode

The essential feature of a Manic Episode is a distinct period during which the predominant mood is either elevated, expansive, or irritable, and there are associated symptoms of the Manic Syndrome. The disturbance is sufficiently severe to cause marked impairment in occupational functioning or in usual social activities or relationships with others, or to require hospitalization to prevent harm to self or others. The associated symptoms include inflated self-esteem or grandiosity (which may be delusional), decreased need for sleep, pressure of speech, flight of ideas, distractibility, increased involvement in goal-directed activity, psychomotor agitation, and excessive involvement in pleasurable activities which have a high potential for painful consequences that the person often does not recognize. The diagnosis is made only if it cannot be established that an organic factor initiated and maintained the disturbance. In addition, the diagnosis is not made if the disturbance is superimposed on Schizophrenia, Schizophreniform Disorder, Delusional Disorder, or Psychotic Disorder NOS, or if the criteria for Schizoaffective Disorder are met.

The elevated mood may be described as euphoric, unusually good, cheerful, or high, often having an infectious quality for the uninvolved observer, but recognized as excessive by those who know the person well. The expansive quality of the mood disturbance is characterized by unceasing and unselective enthusiasm for interacting with people and seeking involvement with other aspects of the environment. Although elevated mood is considered the prototypic symptom, the predominant mood disturbance may be irritability, which may be most apparent when the person is thwarted.

Characteristically, there is inflated self-esteem, ranging from uncritical self-confidence to marked grandiosity, which may be delusional. For instance, the person may give advice on matters about which he or she has no special knowledge, such as how to run a mental hospital or the United Nations. Despite lack of any particular talent, the person may start a novel, compose music, or seek publicity for some impractical invention. Grandiose delusions involving a special relationship to God or some well-known figure from the political, religious, or entertainment world are common.

Almost invariably there is a decreased need for sleep; the person awakens several hours before the usual time, full of energy. When the sleep disturbance is severe, the person may go for days without any sleep at all, yet not feel tired.

Manic speech is typically loud, rapid, and difficult to interrupt. Often it is full of jokes, puns, plays on words, and amusing irrelevancies. It may become theatrical, with dramatic mannerisms and singing. Sounds rather than meaningful conceptual relationships may govern word choice (clanging). If the person's mood is more irritable than expansive, his or her speech may be marked by complaints, hostile comments, and angry tirades.

Frequently there is flight of ideas, i.e., a nearly continuous flow of accelerated speech, with abrupt changes from topic to topic, usually based on understandable associations, distracting stimuli, or plays on words. When flight of ideas is severe, speech may be disorganized and incoherent. However, loosening of associations and incoherence may occur even when there is no flight of ideas, particularly if the person is on medication.

Distractibility is usually present, and is evidenced by rapid changes in speech or activity as a result of responding to various irrelevant external stimuli, such as background noise, or signs or pictures on the wall.

The increase in goal-directed activity often involves excessive planning of, and participation in, multiple activities (e.g., sexual, occupational, political, religious). Almost invariably there is increased sociability, which includes efforts to renew old acquaintanceships and calling friends at all hours of the night. The person does not recognize the intrusive, domineering, and demanding nature of these interactions. Frequently, expansiveness, unwarranted optimism, grandiosity, and lack of judgment lead to such activities as buying sprees, reckless driving, foolish business investments, and sexual behavior unusual for the person. Often the activities have a disorganized, flamboyant, or bizarre quality—for example, dressing in colorful or strange garments, wearing excessive, poorly applied makeup, or distributing candy, money, or advice to passing strangers.

Associated features. Frequently the person does not recognize that he or she is ill and resists all efforts to be treated. Another common associated feature is lability of mood, with rapid shifts to anger or depression. The depression, expressed by tearfulness, suicidal threats, or other depressive symptoms, may last moments, hours, or, more rarely, days. Occasionally the depressive and manic symptoms occur simultaneously, or may alternate rapidly within a few days. Less often, in Bipolar Disorder, Mixed, the depressive symptoms are prominent and last at least a full day, and there is the full symptom picture of both Manic and Major Depressive Episodes.

When delusions or hallucinations are present, their content

is usually clearly consistent with the predominant mood (mood-congruent). God's voice may be heard explaining that the person has a special mission. Persecutory delusions may be based on the idea that the person is being persecuted because of some special relationship or attribute. Less commonly, the content of the hallucinations or delusions has no apparent relationship to the predominant mood (mood-incongruent).

Catatonic symptoms, such as stupor, mutism, negativism, and posturing, may be present.

Age at onset. Retrospective studies indicate that the mean age at onset is in the early 20s. However, some studies indicate that a sizable number of new cases appear after age 50.

Course. Manic Episodes typically begin suddenly, with a rapid escalation of symptoms over a few days. The episodes usually last from a few days to months, and are briefer and end more abruptly than Major Depressive Episodes.

Impairment. By definition, there is considerable impairment in social and occupational functioning. Often there is a need for protection from the consequences of poor judgment and hyperactivity, which often results in involuntary hospitalization.

Complications. The most common complications of a Manic Episode are Psychoactive Substance Abuse and the consequences of actions resulting from impaired judgment, such as financial losses and illegal activities.

Predisposing factors. Frequently Manic Episodes follow psychosocial stressors. Antidepressant somatic treatment (drugs or ECT) may precipitate a Manic Episode. Childbirth sometimes precipitates a Manic Episode.

Differential diagnosis of Manic Episode. The diagnosis is made only when it cannot be established that an organic factor initiated and maintained the disturbance. **Organic Mood Syndromes** with mania may be due to such psychoactive substances as amphetamines or steroids, or to some other known organic factor, such as multiple sclerosis (see discussion of etiologic factors of Organic Mood Syndrome, p. 112). A Manic Episode should be diagnosed in cases that are apparently precipitated by somatic antidepressant treatment (e.g., drugs, ECT). Some investigators consider a postpartum Manic Episode to have an "organic" etiology. However, because of the difficulty of distinguishing the psychological and physiologic stresses associated with pregnancy and delivery, in this classification such episodes are not considered Organic Mood Syndromes, and should be diagnosed as Manic Episodes.

In **Attention-deficit Hyperactivity Disorder** there is persistent excessive activity and restlessness that may suggest a Manic Episode. However, the mood is not abnormally expansive or elevated and the disturbance does not have the relatively clear onset that is characteristic of a Manic Episode.

In **Schizophrenia, Paranoid Type,** there may be irritability, anger, and psychotic symptoms that are difficult to distinguish from similar features of a Manic Episode. In such instances it may be necessary to rely on features that, on a statistical basis, are associated differentially with the two conditions. For example, the diagnosis of a Manic Episode is more likely if there is a family history of Mood Disorder, good premorbid adjustment, and a previous episode of a Mood Disorder from which there was complete recovery.

In **Hypomanic Episodes** the mood disturbance is not sufficiently severe to cause marked impairment in social or occupational functioning or to require hospitalization.

Diagnostic Criteria for Manic Episode

Note: A "Manic Syndrome" is defined as including criteria A, B, and C below. A "Hypomanic Syndrome" is defined as including criteria A and B, but not C, i.e., no marked impairment.

A. A distinct period of abnormally and persistently elevated, expansive, or irritable mood.

B. During the period of mood disturbance, at least three of the following symptoms have persisted (four if the mood is only irritable) and have been present to a significant degree:

(1) inflated self-esteem or grandiosity
(2) decreased need for sleep, e.g., feels rested after only three hours of sleep
(3) more talkative than usual or pressure to keep talking
(4) flight of ideas or subjective experience that thoughts are racing
(5) distractibility, i.e., attention too easily drawn to unimportant or irrelevant external stimuli
(6) increase in goal-directed activity (either socially, at work or school, or sexually) or psychomotor agitation

(7) excessive involvement in pleasurable activities which have a high potential for painful consequences, e.g., the person engages in unrestrained buying sprees, sexual indiscretions, or foolish business investments

C. Mood disturbance sufficiently severe to cause marked impairment in occupational functioning or in usual social activities or relationships with others, or to necessitate hospitalization to prevent harm to self or others.

D. At no time during the disturbance have there been delusions or hallucinations for as long as two weeks in the absence of prominent mood symptoms (i.e., before the mood symptoms developed or after they have remitted).

E. Not superimposed on Schizophrenia, Schizophreniform Disorder, Delusional Disorder, or Psychotic Disorder NOS.

F. It cannot be established that an organic factor initiated and maintained the disturbance. **Note:** Somatic antidepressant treatment (e.g., drugs, ECT) that apparently precipitates a mood disturbance should not be considered an etiologic organic factor.

Manic Episode codes: fifth-digit code numbers and criteria for severity of current state of Bipolar Disorder, Manic or Mixed:

1—Mild: Meets minimum symptom criteria for a Manic Episode (or almost meets symptom criteria if there has been a previous Manic Episode).

2—Moderate: Extreme increase in activity or impairment in judgment.

3—Severe, without Psychotic Features: Almost continual supervision required in order to prevent physical harm to self or others.

4—With Psychotic Features: Delusions, hallucinations, or catatonic symptoms. If possible, **specify** whether the psychotic features are *mood-congruent* or *mood-incongruent*.

Mood-congruent psychotic features: Delusions or hallucinations whose content is entirely consistent with the typical manic themes of inflated worth, power, knowledge, identity, or special relationship to a deity or famous person.

Mood-incongruent psychotic features: Either *(a)* or *(b):*
  (a) Delusions or hallucinations whose content does *not* involve the typical manic themes of inflated worth, power, knowledge, identity, or special relationship to a deity or famous person. Included are such symptoms as persecutory delusions (not directly related to grandiose ideas or themes), thought insertion, and delusions of being controlled.
  (b) Catatonic symptoms, e.g., stupor, mutism, negativism, posturing.

5—In Partial Remission: Full criteria were previously, but are not currently, met: some signs or symptoms of the disturbance have persisted.

6—In Full Remission: Full criteria were previously met, but there have been no significant signs or symptoms of the disturbance for at least two months.

0—Unspecified.

Hypomanic Episode

The essential feature of a Hypomanic Episode is a distinct period in which the predominant mood is either elevated, expansive, or irritable and there are associated symptoms of the Manic Syndrome. By definition, the disturbance is not severe enough to cause marked impairment in social or occupational functioning or to require hospitalization (as required in the diagnosis of a Manic Episode). The associated features of Hypomanic Episodes are similar to those of a Manic Episode except that delusions are never present and all other symptoms tend to be less severe than in Manic Episodes.

Major Depressive Episode

The essential feature of a Major Depressive Episode is either depressed mood (or possibly, in children or adolescents, an irritable mood) or loss of interest or pleasure in all, or almost all, activities, and associated symptoms, for a period of at least two weeks. The symptoms represent a change from previous functioning and are relatively persistent, that is, they occur for most of the day, nearly every day, during at least a two-week period. The associated symptoms include appetite disturbance, change in weight, sleep disturbance, psychomotor agitation or retardation, decreased energy, feelings of worthlessness or excessive or inappropriate guilt, difficulty thinking or concentrating, and recurrent thoughts of death, or suicidal ideation or attempts. The diagnosis is made only if it cannot be established that an organic factor initiated and maintained the disturbance and the disturbance is not the normal reaction to the loss of a loved one (Uncomplicated Bereavement). In addition, the diagnosis is not made if the disturbance is superimposed on Schizophrenia, Schizophreniform Disorder, Delusional Disorder, or Psychotic Disorder NOS, or if the criteria for Schizoaffective Disorder are met.

A person with depressed mood will usually describe feeling depressed, sad, hopeless, discouraged, "down in the dumps," or some other colloquial equivalent. In some cases, although the person may deny feeling depressed, the presence of depressed mood can be inferred from others' observing that the person looks sad or depressed.

Loss of interest or pleasure is probably always present in a Major Depressive Episode to some degree, and is often described by the person as not being as interested in usual activities as previously, "not caring anymore," or, more rarely, a painful inability to experience pleasure. The person may not complain of loss of interest or pleasure, but family members generally will notice withdrawal from friends and family and neglect of avocations that were previously a source of pleasure.

Appetite is frequently disturbed, loss of appetite being the more common, but increased appetite sometimes being evident. When loss of appetite is severe, there may be significant weight loss or, in the case of children, failure to make expected weight gains. When appetite is markedly increased, there may be significant weight gain.

Sleep is commonly disturbed, the more frequent complaint being insomnia, but sometimes hypersomnia. The insomnia may involve difficulty falling asleep (initial insomnia), waking up during sleep and then returning to sleep only with difficulty (middle insomnia), or early morning awakening (terminal insomnia). Hypersomnia may involve sleeping for a longer period of time than is usual, daytime sleepiness, or taking excessive naps. Sometimes the sleep disturbance, rather than the depressed mood or loss of interest or pleasure, is the main symptom that brings the person into treatment (see Sleep Disorders, p. 297).

Psychomotor agitation takes the form of inability to sit still, pacing, hand-wringing, pulling or rubbing of hair, skin, clothing, or other objects. Psychomotor retardation may take the form of slowed speech, increased pauses before answering, soft or monotonous speech, slowed body movements, a markedly decreased amount of speech (poverty of speech), or muteness. A decrease in energy level is almost invariably present, and is experienced as sustained fatigue even in the absence of physical exertion. The smallest task may seem difficult or impossible to accomplish.

The sense of worthlessness varies from feelings of inadequacy to completely unrealistic negative evaluations of one's worth. The person may reproach himself or herself for minor failings that are exaggerated and search the environment for cues confirming the negative self-evaluation. Guilt may be expressed as an excessive reaction to either current or past failings or as exaggerated responsibility for some untoward or tragic event. The sense of worthlessness or guilt may be of delusional proportions.

Difficulty in concentrating, slowed thinking, and indecisiveness are frequent. The person may complain of memory difficulty and appear easily distracted.

Thoughts of death (not just fear of dying) are common. Often there is the belief that the person or others would be better off dead. There may be suicidal thoughts, with or without a specific plan, or suicide attempts.

Associated features.   Commonly associated features include tearfulness, anxiety, irritability, brooding or obsessive rumination, excessive concern with physical health, panic attacks, and phobias.

When delusions or hallucinations are present, their content is usually clearly consistent with the predominant mood (mood-congruent). A common delusion is that one is being persecuted because of a moral transgression or some personal inadequacy. There may be nihilistic delusions of world or personal destruction, somatic delusions of cancer or other serious illness, or delusions of poverty. Hallucinations, when present, are usually transient and not elaborate, and may involve voices that berate the person for his or her shortcomings or sins.

Less commonly the content of the hallucinations or delusions has no apparent relationship to the mood disturbance (mood-incongruent). This is particularly the case with persecutory delusions, in which the person may be at a loss to explain why he or she should be the object of persecution. Less common mood-incongruent psychotic symptoms include thought insertion, thought broadcasting, and delusions of control.

Age-specific features.   Although the essential features of a Major Depressive Episode are similar in children, adolescents, and adults, there are some differences.

In prepubertal children with a Major Depressive Episode, somatic complaints, psychomotor agitation, and mood-congruent hallucinations (usually only a single voice talking to the child) are particularly frequent.

In children with a Major Depressive Episode, Anxiety Disorders of Childhood (Separation Anxiety Disorder, Overanxious Disorder, and Avoidant Disorder of Childhood or Adolescence) and phobias are common.

In adolescents, negativistic or frankly antisocial behavior and use of alcohol or illicit drugs may be present and justify the additional diagnoses of Oppositional Defiant Disorder, Conduct Disorder, or Psychoactive Substance Abuse or Dependence. Feelings of wanting to leave home or of not being understood and approved of, restlessness, grouchiness, and aggression are common. Sulkiness, a reluctance to cooperate in family ventures, and withdrawal from social activities, with retreat to one's room, are frequent. School difficulties are likely. There may be inattention to personal appearance and increased emotionality, with particular sensitivity to rejection in love relationships.

In elderly adults some of the symptoms of depression, e.g., disorientation, memory loss, and distractibility, may suggest Dementia. Loss of interest or pleasure in the person's usual activities may appear as apathy; difficulty in concentration, as inattentiveness. These symptoms make the differential diagnosis of "pseudodementia" (due to depression) from true Dementia (an Organic Mental Disorder) particularly difficult (p. 106).

Age at onset. The average age at onset is in the late 20s, but a Major Depressive Episode may begin at any age, including infancy.

Course. The onset of a Major Depressive Episode is variable, the symptoms usually developing over days to weeks; in some cases, however, it may be sudden (e.g., when associated with severe psychosocial stress). In some instances prodromal symptoms—e.g., generalized anxiety, panic attacks, phobias, or mild depressive symptoms—may occur over a period of several months.

The duration of a Major Depressive Episode is also variable. Untreated, the episode typically lasts six months or longer. Usually there is a complete remission of symptoms, and general functioning returns to the premorbid level; but in a large proportion of cases, some symptoms of the episode persist for as long as two years without a period of two months or longer without significant depressive symptoms. These episodes are specified as *Chronic Type*.

Impairment. In Major Depressive Episodes the degree of impairment varies, but there is always some interference in social and occupational functioning. If impairment is severe, the person may be totally unable to function socially or occupationally, or even to feed or clothe himself or herself or maintain minimal personal hygiene.

Complications. The most serious complication of a Major Depressive Episode is suicide.

Predisposing factors. Chronic physical illness and Psychoactive Substance Dependence, particularly Alcohol and Cocaine Dependence, apparently predispose to the development of a Major Depressive Episode. Frequently a Major Depressive Episode follows a psychosocial stressor, particularly death of a loved one, marital separation, or divorce. Childbirth sometimes precipitates a Major Depressive Episode.

Differential diagnosis of Major Depressive Episode. The diagnosis is made only when it cannot be established that an organic factor initiated and maintained the disturbance. An **Organic Mood Syndrome with depression** may be due to substances such as reserpine, to infectious diseases such as influenza, or to hypothyroidism (see discussion of etiologic factors of Organic Mood Syndrome, p. 112). Some investigators consider a postpartum depressive episode to have an "organic" etiology. However, because of the difficulty of separating the psychological and physiologic stresses associated with pregnancy and delivery, in this classification such episodes are not considered Organic Mood Syndromes, and are diagnosed as Major Depressive Episodes.

Primary Degenerative Dementia of the Alzheimer Type and **Multi-infarct Dementia,** because of the presence of disorientation, apathy, and complaints of difficulty concentrating or of memory loss, may be difficult to distinguish from a Major Depressive Episode occurring in the elderly. If the presenting symptoms suggesting Dementia are significantly more prominent than the depressive ones, then the diagnosis should be **Dementia with depression.** If the symptoms suggesting a Major Depressive Episode are at least as prominent as those suggesting Dementia, it is best to diagnose a Major Depressive Episode and assume that the symptoms suggesting Dementia represent a **pseudodementia** that is a manifestation of the Major Depressive Episode. In such cases the successful treatment of the Major Depressive Episode often results in disappearance of the symptoms suggesting Dementia, which indicates that the appropriate diagnosis was Major Depression. If the symptoms of the Dementia persist, this suggests that the appropriate diagnosis was **Dementia with depression.**

If a **psychological reaction to the functional impairment associated with a physical illness** that does not involve the central nervous system causes a depression that meets the full criteria for a Major Depressive Episode, the Major Depression should be recorded on Axis I, the physical disorder on Axis III, and the severity of the psychosocial stressor on Axis IV. Examples would include the psychological reaction to amputation of a leg or to the development of a life-threatening or incapacitating illness.

In **Schizophrenia** there are usually some depressive symptoms. If an episode of depression is superimposed on the residual phase of Schizophrenia, or if it occurs briefly during the active phase, the additional diagnosis of either Depressive Disorder NOS or Adjustment Disorder with Depressed Mood may be made, but not Major Depression. A person with **Schizophrenia, Catatonic Type,** may appear to be withdrawn and depressed, and it may be difficult to distinguish this condition from Major Depression with psychomotor retardation. An amobarbital interview can often be helpful in making this distinction. However, when the differential is still unclear, it may be necessary to rely on symptoms that, on a statistical basis, are associated differentially with the two disorders. For example, the diagnosis of a Major Depressive Episode is more likely if there is a family history of Mood Disorder, good premorbid adjustment, and a previous episode of mood disturbance from which there was complete recovery.

In **Schizoaffective Disorder** there are periods of at least two weeks during which there have been delusions or hallucinations in the absence of prominent mood disturbance.

Uncomplicated Bereavement is distinguished from a Major Depressive Episode and is not considered a mental disorder even when associated with the full depressive syndrome. However, morbid preoccupation with worthlessness, suicidal ideation, marked functional impairment or psychomotor retardation, or prolonged duration suggests that bereavement is complicated by a Major Depressive Episode.

Diagnostic Criteria
for Major Depressive Episode

Note: A "Major Depressive Syndrome" is defined as criterion A below.

A. At least five of the following symptoms have been present during the same two-week period and represent a change from previous functioning; at least one of the symptoms is either (1) depressed mood, or (2) loss of interest or pleasure. (Do not include symptoms that are clearly due to a physical condition, mood-incongruent delusions or hallucinations, incoherence, or marked loosening of associations.)

(1) depressed mood (or can be irritable mood in children and adolescents) most of the day, nearly every day, as indicated either by subjective account or observation by others

(2) markedly diminished interest or pleasure in all, or almost all, activities most of the day, nearly every day (as indicated either by subjective account or observation by others of apathy most of the time)

(3) significant weight loss or weight gain when not dieting (e.g., more than 5% of body weight in a month), or decrease or increase in appetite nearly every day (in children, consider failure to make expected weight gains)

(4) insomnia or hypersomnia nearly every day

(5) psychomotor agitation or retardation nearly every day (observable by others, not merely subjective feelings of restlessness or being slowed down)

(6) fatigue or loss of energy nearly every day

(7) feelings of worthlessness or excessive or inappropriate guilt (which may be delusional) nearly every day (not merely self-reproach or guilt about being sick)

(8) diminished ability to think or concentrate, or indecisiveness, nearly every day (either by subjective account or as observed by others)

(9) recurrent thoughts of death (not just fear of dying), recurrent suicidal ideation without a specific plan, or a suicide attempt or a specific plan for committing suicide

B. (1) It cannot be established that an organic factor initiated and maintained the disturbance

(2) The disturbance is not a normal reaction to the death of a loved one (Uncomplicated Bereavement)

Note: Morbid preoccupation with worthlessness, suicidal ideation, marked functional impairment or psychomotor retardation, or prolonged duration suggest bereavement complicated by Major Depression.

C. At no time during the disturbance have there been delusions or hallucinations for as long as two weeks in the absence of prominent mood symptoms (i.e., before the mood symptoms developed or after they have remitted).

D. Not superimposed on Schizophrenia, Schizophreniform Disorder, Delusional Disorder, or Psychotic Disorder NOS.

Major Depressive Episode codes: fifth-digit code numbers and criteria for severity of current state of Bipolar Disorder, Depressed, or Major Depression:

1—Mild: Few, if any, symptoms in excess of those required to make the diagnosis, **and** symptoms result in only minor impairment in occupational functioning or in usual social activities or relationships with others.

2—Moderate: Symptoms or functional impairment between ''mild'' and ''severe.''

3—Severe, without Psychotic Features: Several symptoms in excess of those required to make the diagnosis, **and** symptoms markedly interfere with occupational functioning or with usual social activities or relationships with others.

4—With Psychotic Features: Delusions or hallucinations. If possible, **specify** whether the psychotic features are *mood-congruent* or *mood-incongruent*.

Mood-congruent psychotic features: Delusions or hallucinations whose content is entirely consistent with the typical depressive themes of personal inadequacy, guilt, disease, death, nihilism, or deserved punishment.

Mood-incongruent psychotic features: Delusions or hallucinations whose content does *not* involve typical depressive themes of personal inadequacy, guilt, disease, death, nihilism, or deserved punishment. Included here are such symptoms as persecutory delusions (not directly related to depressive themes), thought insertion, thought broadcasting, and delusions of control.

5—In Partial Remission: Intermediate between "In Full Remission" and "Mild," **and** no previous Dysthymia. (If Major Depressive Episode was superimposed on Dysthymia, the diagnosis of Dysthymia alone is given once the full criteria for a Major Depressive Episode are no longer met.)

6—In Full Remission: During the past six months no significant signs or symptoms of the disturbance.

0—Unspecified.

Specify chronic if current episode has lasted two consecutive years without a period of two months or longer during which there were no significant depressive symptoms.

Specify if current episode is **Melancholic Type**.

Diagnostic Criteria
for Melancholic Type

The presence of at least five of the following:

(1) loss of interest or pleasure in all, or almost all, activities
(2) lack of reactivity to usually pleasurable stimuli (does not feel much better, even temporarily, when something good happens)
(3) depression regularly worse in the morning

(4) early morning awakening (at least two hours before usual time of awakening)

(5) psychomotor retardation or agitation (not merely subjective complaints)

(6) significant anorexia or weight loss (e.g., more than 5% of body weight in a month)

(7) no significant personality disturbance before first Major Depressive Episode

(8) one or more previous Major Depressive Episodes followed by complete, or nearly complete, recovery

(9) previous good response to specific and adequate somatic antidepressant therapy, e.g., tricyclics, ECT, MAOI, lithium

---

Diagnostic Criteria for Seasonal Pattern

A. There has been a regular temporal relationship between the onset of an episode of Bipolar Disorder (including Bipolar Disorder NOS) or Recurrent Major Depression (including Depressive Disorder NOS) and a particular 60-day period of the year (e.g., regular appearance of depression between the beginning of October and the end of November).

Note: Do not include cases in which there is an obvious effect of seasonally related psychosocial stressors, e.g., regularly being unemployed every winter.

B. Full remissions (or a change from depression to mania or hypomania) also occurred within a particular 60-day period of the year (e.g., depression disappears from mid-February to mid-April).

C. There have been at least three episodes of mood disturbance in three separate years that demonstrated the temporal seasonal relationship defined in A and B; at least two of the years were consecutive.

D. Seasonal episodes of mood disturbance, as described above, outnumbered any nonseasonal episodes of such disturbance that may have occurred by more than three to one.

BIPOLAR DISORDERS

296.6x Bipolar Disorder, Mixed
296.4x Bipolar Disorder, Manic
296.5x Bipolar Disorder, Depressed

The essential feature of Bipolar Disorder is one or more Manic Episodes (see p. 214), usually accompanied by one or more Major Depressive Episodes (see p. 218).

Bipolar Disorder is subclassified in the fourth digit as either mixed, manic, or depressed, depending on the clinical features of the current episode (or most recent episode if the disorder is currently in partial or full remission). In addition, Bipolar Disorder is subclassified in the fifth digit according to the current state of the disturbance. If the criteria are currently met for a Manic Episode or Major Depressive Episode, the severity of the episode is indicated as either mild, moderate, severe without psychotic features, or with psychotic features. If the criteria are not currently met, the fifth digit indicates whether the disturbance is in partial or full remission.

Course. In Bipolar Disorder the initial episode that occasioned hospitalization is usually manic. Both the Manic and Major Depressive Episodes are more frequent than the Major Depressive Episodes in Major Depression, Recurrent. Frequently a Manic or Major Depressive Episode is immediately followed by a short episode of the other kind. In many cases there are two or more complete cycles (a Manic and a Major Depressive Episode that succeed each other without a period of remission) within a year. Such cases have been called "rapid cycling." In rare cases over long periods of time, there is an alternation of the two kinds of episodes without any intervening period of normal mood.

There is evidence that cases of Bipolar Disorder with a mixed or rapid cycling episode have a much more chronic course than those without this type of episode.

Prevalence. It is estimated that from 0.4% to 1.2% of the adult population have had Bipolar Disorder.

Sex ratio. Recent epidemiologic studies in the United States indicate that the disorder is equally common in males and in females (unlike Major Depression, which is more common in females).

Familial pattern. Bipolar Disorder has clearly been shown to occur at much higher rates in first-degree biologic relatives of people with Bipolar Disorder than in the general population.

Differential diagnosis. In **Cyclothymia** there are numerous periods of Hypomanic Episodes and numerous periods of depressed mood or loss of interest or pleasure that do not meet the criteria for a Major Depressive Episode. If a Manic Episode occurs after the first two years of Cyclothymia, the additional diagnosis of Bipolar Disorder is given.

Diagnostic Criteria
for Bipolar Disorders

296.6x Bipolar Disorder, Mixed

For fifth digit, use the Manic Episode codes (p. 218) to describe current state.

A. Current (or most recent) episode involves the full symptomatic picture of both Manic and Major Depressive Episodes (except for the duration requirement of two weeks for depressive symptoms) (p. 217 and p. 222), intermixed or rapidly alternating every few days.

B. Prominent depressive symptoms lasting at least a full day.

Specify if **seasonal pattern** (see p. 224).

296.4x Bipolar Disorder, Manic

For fifth digit, use the Manic Episode codes (p. 218) to describe current state.

Currently (or most recently) in a Manic Episode (p. 217). (If there has been a previous Manic Episode, the current episode need not meet the full criteria for a Manic Episode.)

Specify if **seasonal pattern** (see p. 224).

296.5x Bipolar Disorder, Depressed

For fifth digit, use the Major Depressive Episode codes (p. 223) to describe current state.

A. Has had one or more Manic Episodes (p. 217).

B. Currently (or most recently) in a Major Depressive Episode (p. 222). (If there has been a previous Major Depressive Episode, the current episode need not meet the full criteria for a Major Depressive Episode.)

Specify if **seasonal pattern** (see p. 224).

301.13 Cyclothymia

The essential feature of this disorder is a chronic mood disturbance, of at least two years' duration (one year for children and adolescents), involving numerous Hypomanic Episodes and numerous periods of depressed mood or loss of interest or pleasure of insufficient severity or duration to meet the criteria for a Major Depressive or a Manic Episode. In order to make the diagnosis, there must be a two-year period (one year for children and adolescents) in which the person is never without hypomanic or depressive symptoms for more than two months. The diagnosis is not made if there is clear evidence of either a Manic Episode or a Major Depressive Episode during the first two years of the disturbance. (A Manic Episode would indicate Bipolar Disorder; a Major Depressive Episode, without a Manic Episode, would indicate Bipolar Disorder NOS.) In addition, the diagnosis is not made if the disturbance is superimposed on a chronic psychotic disorder, such as Schizophrenia or Delusional Disorder, or if it is initiated and maintained by a specific organic factor or substance.

The boundaries between Cyclothymia and Bipolar Disorder and Bipolar Disorder NOS are not well defined, and some investigators believe that Cyclothymia is a mild form of Bipolar Disorder.

Associated features.   Associated features are similar to those of Manic Episode (p. 216) and Major Depressive Episode (p. 220) except that, by definition, there is no marked impairment in social or occupational functioning during the Hypomanic Episodes. In fact, in some cases the person is particularly productive in occupational situations and socially effective during Hypomanic Episodes. However, many people experience social difficulties in their interpersonal relationships and academic and occupational pursuits because of the recurrent cycles of mood swings.

Psychoactive Substance Abuse is common as a result of self-treatment with sedatives and alcohol during the depressed periods and the self-indulgent use of stimulants and psychedelic substances during the hypomanic periods.

Age at onset.   The disorder usually begins in adolescence or early adult life.

Course.   The disorder usually is without clear onset and has a chronic course. Often the person develops Bipolar Disorder.

Impairment. During periods of depression, social and occupational functioning are invariably impaired, although not as severely as in a Major Depressive Episode.

Complications. See Manic Episode (p. 216) and Major Depressive Episode (p. 221). Frequently Manic and Major Depressive Episodes are complications of this disorder.

Predisposing factors. No information.

Prevalence. Studies have reported a lifetime prevalence of from 0.4% to 3.5%.

Sex ratio. In clinical samples the disorder is apparently equally common in males and in females.

Familial pattern. Major Depression and Bipolar Disorder may be more common among first-degree biologic relatives of people with Cyclothymia than among the general population.

Differential diagnosis. See differential diagnosis of a Manic Episode (p. 216). If a Manic Episode or a Major Depressive Episode occurs during the first two years of what appears to be Cyclothymia, the diagnosis of either **Bipolar Disorder** (for a Manic Episode) or **Bipolar Disorder NOS** (for a Major Depressive Episode) is given. In **Borderline Personality Disorder** there are often marked shifts in mood, from depression to irritability or anxiety, that may suggest Hypomanic Episodes. However, the characteristic associated symptoms of a Hypomanic Episode, such as less need for sleep and racing thoughts, are rarely present.

Diagnostic Criteria for 301.13
Cyclothymia

A. For at least two years (one year for children and adolescents), presence of numerous Hypomanic Episodes (all of the criteria for a Manic Episode, p. 217, except criterion C that indicates marked impairment) and numerous periods with depressed mood or loss of interest or pleasure that did not meet criterion A of Major Depressive Episode.

B. During a two-year period (one year in children and adolescents) of the disturbance, never without hypomanic or depressive symptoms for more than two months at a time.

C. No clear evidence of a Major Depressive Episode or Manic Episode during the first two years of the disturbance (or one year in children and adolescents).

Note: After this minimum period of Cyclothymia, there may be superimposed Manic or Major Depressive Episodes, in which case the additional diagnosis of Bipolar Disorder or Bipolar Disorder NOS should be given.

D. Not superimposed on a chronic psychotic disorder, such as Schizophrenia or Delusional Disorder.

E. It cannot be established that an organic factor initiated and maintained the disturbance, e.g., repeated intoxication from drugs or alcohol.

296.70 Bipolar Disorder Not Otherwise Specified

Disorders with manic or hypomanic features that do not meet the criteria for any specific Bipolar Disorder.

Examples:

(1) at least one Hypomanic Episode and at least one Major Depressive Episode, but never either a Manic Episode or Cyclothymia. Such cases have been referred to as "Bipolar II."

(2) one or more Hypomanic Episodes, but without Cyclothymia or a history of either a Manic or a Major Depressive Episode

(3) a Manic Episode superimposed on Delusional Disorder, residual Schizophrenia, or Psychotic Disorder NOS

Specify if **seasonal pattern** (see p. 224).

DEPRESSIVE DISORDERS

296.2x Major Depression, Single Episode
296.3x Major Depression, Recurrent

The essential feature of Major Depression is one or more Major Depressive Episodes (see p. 218) without a history of either a Manic Episode (see p. 214) or an unequivocal Hypomanic Episode. Major Depression is subclassified in the fourth digit as either Single Episode or Recurrent. In addition, it is subclassified in the fifth digit to indicate the current state of the disturbance. If the criteria are currently met for a Major Depressive Episode, the severity of the episode is indicated as either mild, moderate, severe without psychotic features, or with psychotic features. If these criteria are not currently met, the fifth digit indicates whether the disturbance is in partial or full remission.

Course. Some people have only a single episode, with full return to premorbid functioning. However, it is estimated that over 50% of people who initially have Major Depression, Single Episode, will eventually have another Major Depressive Episode, the illness then meeting the criteria for Major Depression, Recurrent. People with Major Depression, Recurrent, are at greater risk of developing Bipolar Disorder than are those with a single episode of Major Depression. People with Major Depression superimposed on Dysthymia (often referred to as "double depression") are at greater risk for having a recurrence of a Major Depressive Episode than those who have only Major Depression.

The course of Major Depression, Recurrent, is variable. Some people have episodes separated by many years of normal functioning; others have clusters of episodes; and still others have increasingly frequent episodes as they grow older. Functioning usually returns to the premorbid level between episodes. In 20% to 35% of cases, however, there is a chronic course, with considerable residual symptomatic and social impairment. Some of these cases continue to meet the criteria for a Major Depressive Episode throughout the course of the disturbance (specified as *Chronic Type*); the others are coded as being in partial remission.

Prevalence. Studies of Major Depression in the United States and Europe, using criteria similar to those in this manual, report a wide range of values for the proportion of the adult population that has had the disorder. The range for females is from 9% to 26%; that for males, 5% to 12%. Studies examining the proportion of the adult population that currently has the disorder report rates ranging from 4.5% to 9.3% for females and 2.3% to 3.2% for males.

There is evidence that prevalence of the disorder has increased in the age cohorts that came to maturity after the Second World War.

Sex ratio.   In almost all studies of Major Depression in adults in industrialized countries, the disorder is estimated to be twice as common in females as in males (unlike Bipolar Disorder, which is equally common in males and in females).

Familial pattern.   Most family studies have shown that Major Depression is 1.5 to 3 times more common among first-degree biologic relatives of people with this disorder than among the general population.

Differential diagnosis.   See differential diagnosis of a Major Depressive Episode (p. 221). A history of a **Manic Episode** or an **unequivocal Hypomanic Episode** precludes the diagnosis of Major Depression. In the first two years of **Dysthymia** (or one year for children and adolescents), there is no clear evidence of a Major Depressive Episode. However, later in the course of Dysthymia, or before its onset, there may be Major Depression.

Diagnostic Criteria
for Major Depression

296.2x Major Depression, Single Episode

For fifth digit, use the Major Depressive Episode codes (p. 223) to describe current state.

A. A single Major Depressive Episode (p. 222).

B. Has never had a Manic Episode (p. 217) or an unequivocal Hypomanic Episode (see p. 217).

Specify if **seasonal pattern** (see p. 224).

296.3x Major Depression, Recurrent

For fifth digit, use the Major Depressive Episode codes (p. 223) to describe current state.

A. Two or more Major Depressive Episodes (p. 222), each separated by at least two months of return to more or less usual functioning. (If there has been a previous Major Depressive Episode, the current episode of depression need not meet the full criteria for a Major Depressive Episode.)

B. Has never had a Manic Episode (p. 217) or an unequivocal Hypomanic Episode (see p. 217).

Specify if **seasonal pattern** (see p. 224).

300.40 Dysthymia (or Depressive Neurosis)

The essential feature of this disorder is a chronic disturbance of mood involving depressed mood (or possibly an irritable mood in children or adolescents), for most of the day more days than not, for at least two years (one year for children and adolescents). In addition, during these periods of depressed mood there are some of the following associated symptoms: poor appetite or overeating, insomnia or hypersomnia, low energy or fatigue, low self-esteem, poor concentration or difficulty making decisions, and feelings of hopelessness.

In order to make the diagnosis, there must be a two-year (one-year for children or adolescents) period in which the person is never without depressive symptoms for more than two months. The diagnosis is not made if there is clear evidence of a Major Depressive Episode during this minimum period of the disturbance. In addition, the diagnosis is not made if the disturbance is superimposed on a chronic psychotic disorder, such as Schizophrenia or Delusional Disorder, or if the disturbance is sustained by a specific organic factor or substance, for example, prolonged administration of an antihypertensive medication.

Dysthymia frequently seems to be a consequence of a pre-existing, chronic, nonmood Axis I or Axis III disorder, e.g., Anorexia Nervosa, Somatization Disorder, Psychoactive Substance Dependence, an Anxiety Disorder, or rheumatoid arthritis. Such cases of Dysthymia are specified as *Secondary Type*; cases of Dysthymia that are apparently not related to a preexisting chronic disorder are specified as *Primary Type*. Cases of Dysthymia that develop before the age of 21 are specified as *early onset*; cases that develop at or after age 21 are specified as *late onset*. Some investigators believe that the early onset primary type represents a distinct nosologic entity.

The boundaries of Dysthymia with Major Depression are unclear, particularly in children and adolescents.

Associated features. Associated features (and age-specific associated features) are similar to those of Major Depressive Episode (p. 220), except that by definition there are no delusions or hallucinations.

Often an associated personality disturbance warrants an additional diagnosis of a Personality Disorder on Axis II.

Age at onset. This disorder usually begins in childhood, adolescence, or early adult life, and for this reason has often been referred to as Depressive Personality.

Course. The disorder usually begins without clear onset and has a chronic course. In clinical settings, people with this disorder usually have superimposed Major Depression, which often is the reason for the person's currently seeking treatment.

Impairment and complications. The impairment in social and occupational functioning is usually mild or moderate because of the chronicity rather than the severity of the depressive syndrome. Therefore, hospitalization is rarely required unless there is a suicide attempt or a superimposed

Major Depression. The complications are similar to those of Major Depression, although, because of the chronicity of this disorder, there may be a greater likelihood of developing Psychoactive Substance Dependence or Abuse.

In children and adolescents, social interaction with peers and adults is frequently affected. Children with depression often react negatively or shyly to praise and frequently respond to positive relationships with negative behaviors (sometimes as testing, sometimes as manifestations of unexpressed resentment and anger). School performance and progress may be deleteriously affected.

Predisposing factors. By definition, predisposing factors for the *secondary type* include chronic nonmood Axis I and Axis III disorders. In addition, chronic psychosocial stressors may predispose to both *primary* and *secondary* types.

In children and adolescents, predisposing factors are the presence of Attention-deficit Hyperactivity Disorder, Conduct Disorder, Mental Retardation, a severe Specific Developmental Disorder, or an inadequate, disorganized, rejecting, and chaotic environment.

Prevalence. This disorder is apparently common.

Sex ratio. Among adults the disorder is apparently more common in females. In children it seems to occur equally frequently in both sexes.

Familial pattern. There is evidence that the disorder is more common among first-degree biologic relatives of people with Major Depression than among the general population.

Differential diagnosis. The differential diagnosis of Dysthymia and Major Depression is particularly difficult, since the two disorders share similar symptoms and differ only in duration and severity.

Usually Major Depression consists of one or more discrete Major Depressive Episodes that can be distinguished from the person's usual functioning, whereas Dysthymia is characterized by a chronic mild depressive syndrome that has been present for many years. When Dysthymia is of many years' duration, the mood disturbance cannot be distinguished from the person's "usual" functioning. If the initial onset of what appears to be Dysthymia directly follows a Major Depressive Episode, the correct diagnosis is **Major Depression in Partial Remission**. The diagnosis of Dysthymia can be made following Major Depression only if there has been a full remission of the Major Depressive Episode lasting at least six months before the development of Dysthymia.

People with Dysthymia frequently have a superimposed Major Depression (often referred to as "double depression"). When a Major Depression is superimposed on preexisting Dysthymia (which has been present for at least two years), both diagnoses should be recorded since it is likely that the person will continue to have Dysthymia after he or she has recovered from the Major Depression.

Often there is evidence of a coexisting personality disturbance. When a person meets the criteria for both Dysthymia and a **Personality Disorder**, both diagnoses should be made. This disorder is particularly common in people with Borderline, Histrionic, Narcissistic, Avoidant, and Dependent Personality Disorders.

Normal fluctuations of mood are not as frequent or severe as the depressed mood in Dysthymia, and there is no interference with social functioning.

Diagnostic Criteria for 300.40
Dysthymia

A. Depressed mood (or can be irritable mood in children and adolescents) for most of the day, more days than not, as indicated either by subjective account or observation by others, for at least two years (one year for children and adolescents).

B. Presence, while depressed, of at least two of the following:

   (1) poor appetite or overeating
   (2) insomnia or hypersomnia
   (3) low energy or fatigue
   (4) low self-esteem
   (5) poor concentration or difficulty making decisions
   (6) feelings of hopelessness

C. During a two-year period (one-year for children and adolescents) of the disturbance, never without the symptoms in A for more than two months at a time.

D. No evidence of an unequivocal Major Depressive Episode during the first two years (one year for children and adolescents) of the disturbance.

Note: There may have been a previous Major Depressive Episode, provided there was a full remission (no significant signs or symptoms for six months) before development of the Dysthymia. In addition, after these two years (one year in children or adolescents) of Dysthymia, there may be superimposed episodes of Major Depression, in which case both diagnoses are given.

E. Has never had a Manic Episode (p. 217) or an unequivocal Hypomanic Episode (see p. 217).

F. Not superimposed on a chronic psychotic disorder, such as Schizophrenia or Delusional Disorder.

G. It cannot be established that an organic factor initiated and maintained the disturbance, e.g., prolonged administration of an antihypertensive medication.

Specify primary or secondary type:

Primary type: the mood disturbance is not related to a preexisting, chronic, nonmood, Axis I or Axis II disorder, e.g., Anorexia Nervosa, Somatization Disorder, a Psychoactive Substance Dependence Disorder, an Anxiety Disorder, or rheumatoid arthritis.

Secondary type: the mood disturbance is apparently related to a preexisting, chronic, nonmood Axis I or Axis III disorder.

Specify early onset or late onset:

Early onset: onset of the disturbance before age 21.

Late onset: onset of the disturbance at age 21 or later.

311.00 Depressive Disorder Not Otherwise Specified

Disorders with depressive features that do not meet the criteria for any specific Mood Disorder or Adjustment Disorder with Depressed Mood.

Examples:

(1) a Major Depressive Episode superimposed on residual Schizophrenia
(2) a recurrent, mild, depressive disturbance that does not meet the criteria for Dysthymia
(3) non-stress-related depressive episodes that do not meet the criteria for a Major Depressive Episode

Specify if **seasonal pattern** (see p. 224).

Index

Page numbers printed in **boldface** type
refer to tables or figures.

Adalat, 72
Addictiveness, 26, 96
Addison's disease, 24
Adolescents
    diagnosing depression in,
      90–91
    suicide of, 19, 91
    symptoms of depression in,
      127
Aerobic exercise, 82
Affect. *See* Mood
Agitation, 3, 33, 64, 78, 125
Alcohol abuse, 54
    suicide and, 41
Allergies, 23–24
Alprazolam, 76
Alzheimer's disease, 21, 129
Amitid, 56, **57**

Amitriptyline, 56, **57**
    in combination drugs, 75–76
Amoxapine, 56, 78
Anafranil, 99
Anatomy of Melancholy, 4
Antianxiety drugs, 76
Anticonvulsants, 75
    during pregnancy, 89–90
Antidepressants, 44, 53–76,
    108–9. *See also* Cyclic
    antidepressants; Lithium;
    Monoamine oxidase
    inhibitors
    alprazolam, 76
    benefits of, 95
    in breast milk, 90
    for children, 91
    classes of, 54

Antidepressants (*cont.*)
combinations of, 55, 75
for conditions other than depression, 99–100
cost of, 67
cyclic, 54–67, **57**
duration of treatment with, 88–89
effect on suicidal thoughts, 67
effectiveness of, 25–26, 55–56
for elderly, 21, 91–92
failure of, 55, 87–88
indications for, 53
informing doctors that patient is on, 94–95
lithium, 73
measuring blood level of, 61, 93–94
mechanism of action of, 17–18
missed doses of, 88
monoamine oxidase inhibitors, 54, 67–73
no addiction to, 26, 96
other medications used with, 73–76
during pregnancy, 89–90
psychotherapy and, 52, 95–96
safety of, 54–55, 96–97
side effects of, 55, 92, 98–99
as sign of weakness, 87
suicide and, 67, 98
switching between, 65
symptoms helped by, 26
taking other drugs while on, 93
taking regularly, 60–61, 88
therapeutic level of, 37
undertreatment with, 55
Antihypertensive drugs, 11
Antipsychotics, 56
Anxiety, 2, 19

Anxiety disorders of childhood, 127
Appetite disturbances, 4, 65, 124
Asendin, 56, 78
Ativan, 76
Attention-deficit hyperactivity disorder, 119, 149
Aventyl, **57**
Avoidant disorder of childhood or adolescence, 127

Beck Depression Inventory, 28
Bedwetting, 99
Behavior changes, 3
Behavior therapy, 51
Benzodiazepines, 76
Bereavement, 1, 10–11, 13, 33, 124, 132
Bicycling, 82
Bipolar disorder, 12–13, 136–45. *See also* Cyclothymia
anticonvulsants for, 75
course of, 137–38
diagnostic criteria for, 138–39
differential diagnosis of, 137–38
essential feature of, 136–37
familial pattern of, 137
lithium for, 73
not otherwise specified, 143
prevalence of, 137
sex ratio of, 137
subclassification of, 113–14, 136
Birth control pills, 11, 24
Blame for depression, 86–87
Blood pressure medications, 11
Blood tests, 36–37
"Blues," 1, 13, 27, 87
Blurred vision, 58, 59
Bodily functions, 3
Books about depression, 103–6
Brain chemicals, 18, 62, 81, 108

Breast-feeding, 90
Bupropion, 56, **57**, 62, 66
Burton, Robert, 4
Buspirone (BuSpar), 74

Carbamazepine, 75
    during pregnancy, 90
Catatonic symptoms
    in manic episode, 118
    in schizophrenia, 130
Causes of depression, 9–11, 15,
        108, 128
    brain chemicals, 18
    combination of, 9–10
    difficult relationships, 10–11
    early losses, 10
    environmental, 11
    genetic, 10, 18
    life events, 18–19, 87
    medical illnesses, 11, 22–24
    medications, 11, 24
    religious preoccupations, 11
Centrax, 76
Chance of developing depression,
        12–13, 18–20
Chemical imbalance, 17–18, 62
Children
    antidepressants for, 91
    anxiety disorders in, 127
    of depressed parents, 10
    diagnosing depression in,
        90–91
    suicide in, 91
    symptoms of depression in,
        19, 90, 126, 149
Chlordiazepoxide, 76
Chlorpromazine, 55, 72
Chronic depression, 114, 127–28
Chronic fatigue syndrome, 22–23
Clomipramine, 99
Clorazepate, 76
Cognition, 2–3
Cognitive behavior therapy, 48–50

Colace, 63
Computed tomography (CT), 36
Conduct disorder, 127, 149
Constipation, 3, 58, 59, 63
Correctol, 63
Cortisone, 11, 24
Cushing's syndrome, 24
Cyclic antidepressants, 54–67, **57**,
        87. *See also*
        Antidepressants
    combined with lithium, 65, 73
    dealing with side effects of,
        62–66
    dosage of, **57**, 58, 61
    generic and trade names of,
        56, **57**, 66–67
    how long until they work, 60
    mechanism of action of, 62
    newer compared with older
        drugs, 66
    questions about, 60–67
    side effects of, 58–66, **57**
    switching between, 65
    switching to/from monoamine
        oxidase inhibitor, 65
    taking regularly, 60–61, 88
Cyclothymia, 113, 139–42
    age at onset of, 140
    associated features in, 140–41
    complications of, 141
    course of, 140
    diagnostic criteria for, 141
    differential diagnosis of, 141
    essential feature of, 139
    familial pattern of, 141
    impairment in, 141
    prevalence of, 141
    sex ratio of, 141
    symptoms of, 140

Dancing, 82
*Darkness Visible: A Memoir of
    Madness*, 9

DDS, 63
Death, 10
Definition of depression, 1
Delusional disorder, 113, 124
Delusions
    in depression, 3, 19, 35, 126
    in manic episode, 118, 122
Dementia, 21, 129
Depakote, 75
    during pregnancy, 90
Depression After Delivery, 21
Depression/Awareness,
    Recognition and Treatment
    Program, 101
Depressive spectrum, 13, **14**
Descriptions of depression, 3–9
Desipramine, **57**, 62
Desyrel, 56, **57**, 66
Dexamethasone suppression test
    (DEX, DST), 37
Dextroamphetamine (Dexedrine),
    74
Diagnosis of depression, 27–38,
    108
    in children and adolescents,
      90–91
    criteria for, 32–35, 131–34,
      146
    differential diagnosis, 128–31
    "hidden" depression, 53, 108
    laboratory tests for, 36–37
    questionnaires for, 29–31
Diagnostic and Statistical Manual
    of Mental Disorders, Third
    Edition, Revised (DSM-III-
    R), 32–36, 111–53
Dialose, 63
Diarrhea, 3
Diazepam, 76
Diet
    lithium and, 92
    monoamine oxidase inhibitors
      and, 68–69, **70–71**, 92

Distractibility, 116
Dizziness, 58, 59, 63–64, 68
Doctors, 85–86
"Double depression," 150
Doxepin, **57**
Drowsiness, 58, 64, 68
Drug abuse, 54
    suicide and, 41
Dry mouth, 3, 58, 59, 62–63
Dynamic psychotherapy, 46–47
Dysthymia, 114, 147–52
    age at onset of, 148
    associated features of, 148
    causes of, 147
    complications of, 148–49
    course of, 148
    diagnostic criteria for, 151–52
    differential diagnosis of, 150
    early- vs. late-onset, 148, 152
    essential feature of, 147
    familial pattern of, 149
    impairment due to, 148–49
    personality disorders and, 150
    predisposing factors for, 149
    prevalence of, 149
    primary vs. secondary, 148,
      152
    sex ratio of, 149
    symptoms of, 147

Early losses, 10
Early morning awakening, 3
Effer-Syllium, 63
Elavil, 56, **57**
Elderly persons
    antidepressants for, 91–92
    depression in, 21–22
    drug side effects in, 59–60
    suicide rate for, 40
    symptoms of depression in,
      129
Electroconvulsive therapy (ECT),
    44, 77–79

brief-pulse, 78
effectiveness of, 77–78
indications for, 55, 77–78
mechanism of action of, 17–18
memory loss due to, 78–79
number of treatments with, 79
use in medically ill patients, 78
Electroencephalogram (EEG), 36
Endep, 56, **57**
Endorphins, 81
Energy loss, 3, 33, 125
Environmental factors, 11
Etrafon, 75
Exercise, 25, 82, 93

Fatigue, 3, 22–23, 33
Fear, 2, 53
Fiberall, 63
Flight of ideas, 116
Fluoxetine, 56, **57**, 58, 65
mechanism of action of, 62
suicide and, 98
switching to monoamine oxidase inhibitor from, 65
Food allergies, 23–24

Gastrointestinal symptoms, 3
Generic drugs, 56, **57**, 66–67
Genetic factors, 10, 18, 108
Grief, 1, 11, 13, 33
Guilt, 33

Haig, Alexander, 5
Hallucinations
in depression, 2–3, 19, 35, 126
in manic episode, 117–18, 122
Haloperidol (Haldol), 56
Hamilton Depression Rating Scale, 28

Hamlet, 4
Headache, 59
Heart palpitations, 58, 59
Helplessness, 2
Hepatitis, 11
"Hidden" depression, 53, 108
Hippocrates, 4
Historical descriptions of depression, 4–9
Hopelessness, 2, 28
Hormone imbalances, 24
Hospitalization, 13, 40
Hydrocil, 63
Hypersomnia, 3, 33, 124
Hyperthyroidism, 24
Hypoglycemia, 23
Hypomanic episode, 120, 123
Hypotension, 58, 59, 63–64, 68
Hypothyroidism, 24, 99

Imipramine, 50, 56, **57**
Impatience, 12
Impulsivity, 12
Influenza, 11
Inheritance, 10, 18, 108
Insomnia, 33, 58, 124–25
Interpersonal psychotherapy, 48
Irritability, 12
Isocarboxazid, 68, **68**

Janimine, 56, **57**

Kidney disorders, 99

Laboratory tests for depression, 36–37
Laxatives, 63
Learning about depression, 100–1
Librium, 76
Life events, 18, 87
Life expectancy, 21
Light therapy, 82–83
Lightheadedness, 58, 59, 63–64, 68

Limbitrol, 75
Lincoln, Abraham, 8–9
Lithium, 13, 54
   antidepressants used with, 65, 73
   diet and, 92
   late-appearing side effects of, 99
   measuring blood level of, 93–94
   during pregnancy, 89–90
Lithium and Manic Depression: A Guide, 73
Logan, Joshua, 7–8
Loneliness, 10
Lorazepam, 76
Loss of interest in activities, 3, 33, 124
Low blood sugar, 23
Ludiomil, 56, **57**

Magnetic resonance imaging (MRI), 36
Major depression, 143–47. *See also* Dysthymia
   course of, 144
   diagnostic criteria for, 32–36, 146
   differential diagnosis of, 145
   in elderly, 21–22
   essential feature of, 143
   familial pattern of, 145
   number of depressive episodes, 12
   in partial remission, 150
   prevalence of, 144–45
   sex ratio of, 145
   symptoms of, 143–44
Major depressive episode, 113, 123–34
   in adolescents, 127
   age at onset of, 127
   associated features in, 126
   associated with physical illness, 129–30
   in children, 127
   chronic type, 114, 128
   complications of, 128
   course of, 127–28
   diagnostic criteria for, 131–34
   differential diagnosis of, 128–31
   duration of, 128
   in elderly, 127
   essential feature of, 123
   impairment in, 128
   melancholic type, 114, 134–35
   predisposing factors for, 128
   seasonal pattern, 135–36
   symptoms of, 123–26
Manic-depression. *See* Bipolar disorder
Manic episode, 12–13, 115–23
   age at onset of, 118
   associated features in, 117–18
   complications of, 118
   course of, 118
   diagnostic criteria for, 120–23
   differential diagnosis of, 119
   elevated mood of, 115–16
   essential feature of, 115
   impairment in, 118
   predisposing factors for, 118–19
   symptoms of, 115–18
Maprotiline, 56, **57**
Marplan, 68, **68**
Medical illnesses causing depression, 11, 22–24
   in elderly, 21
   use of electroconvulsive therapy in, 78–79
Medications causing depression, 11, 24
Melancholic depression, 114, 134–35

Melancholy, 4
Memory impairment, 125
  due to antidepressants, 58, 59
  due to electroconvulsive
    therapy, 78–79
Menstruation, 24–25
Metamucil, 63
Methylphenidate, 74
Migraine, 99
Mineral supplements, 92–93
Missed doses, 88
Moi-Stir, 63
Monoamine oxidase inhibitors, 54,
  67–72. *See also*
    Antidepressants
  combined with lithium, 65,
    73–74
  dosage of, **68**
  hypertensive reaction in
    patients on, 69, 72
    antidotes for, 72
    diet and, 69, **70–71**, 92
    headache of, 69, 72
    symptoms of, 71
    treatment of, 72
  measuring blood level of,
    93–94
  mechanism of action of, 67
  questions about, 69, 72
  side effects of, 68
  switching to/from cyclic
    antidepressants, 65
  using other medications while
    on, 69, **71**
Mononucleosis, 11
Mood
  depressed, 2, 32–33, 123
  manic, 12, 115–16
Mood disorders, 112–13
  bipolar, 138–45
  depressive, 143–52
  subclassification of, 113–15
  terminology of, 112–13
Mood episodes, 113

  hypomanic, 120, 123
  major depressive, 123–34
  manic, 115–23
Mood syndromes, 111–15
Multi-infarct dementia, 129

Nardil, 68, **68**
National Alliance for the Mentally
  Ill, 101
National Depressive and Manic-
  Depressive Association,
  100
Nausea, 4, 59
Navane, 56
Negative thinking, 2, 33, 123–24
  cognitive behavior therapy
    for, 48–50
Nervousness, 64
Neurosurgery, 84
Neurotransmitters, 18, 62, 81, 108
Nifedipine, 72
Norepinephrine, 18, 62
Norpramin, **57**, 62
Nortriptyline, **57**

Obsessive-compulsive disorder, 19,
  53–54, 100
Oppositional defiant disorder, 127
Oral contraceptives, 11, 24
Orex, 63
Organic mood syndrome, 113
  with depression, 129
  with mania, 119
Orthostatic hypotension, 58, 59,
  63–64, 68
Overanxious disorder, 127
Oxazepam, 76

Pain, 3
Pamelor, **57**
Panic disorder, 19, 53, 99
Parathyroid abnormalities, 24
Parnate, 68, **68**
"Pep pills," 26, 96

Perphenazine, 75
Pertofrane, **57**, 62
Phenelzine, 68, **68**
Phobias, 19, 99–100
Phototherapy, 82–83
Physicians, 85–86
Pilocarpine, 63
Placebo studies, 50
Positron-emission tomography
    (PET), 37
Postpartum depression, 20–21
Prazepam, 76
Prednisone, 24
Pregnancy, 89–90
Premenstrual syndrome, 24–25
Prevalence
    of bipolar disorder, 137
    of cyclothymia, 141
    of depression, 12–13, 18–19,
        144–45
    of dysthymia, 150
    of suicide, 39–40
Procardia, 72
Protriptyline, **57**
Prozac, 56, **57**, 58, 65
    mechanism of action of,
        62
    suicide and, 98
    switching to monoamine
        oxidase inhibitor from, 65
Pseudodementia, 21, 129
Psychiatrists, 86
Psychologists, 86
Psychosurgery, 84
Psychotherapy, 26, 43, 45–52,
    109
    antidepressants and, 52,
        95–96
    behavior therapy, 51
    cognitive-behavioral therapy,
        48–50
    definition of, 45
    dynamic, 46–47

    effectiveness of, 45–46,
        51–52
    interpersonal, 48
    short-term, 47
    supportive, 43, 46
Psychotic depression, 3
    amoxapine for, 78
    combination drugs for, 75–76
    electroconvulsive therapy for,
        77–79
    treatment of, 55–56
Pyridoxine deficiency, 24, 93

Regutol, 63
Relationship difficulties, 10
    interpersonal psychotherapy
        for, 48
Religion, 11
Restlessness, 64, 68
"Retarded" depression, 3, 33, 125
Risk factors for depression, 9–11
Ritalin, 74
Rowing, 82
Running, 82

Sadness, 1–4, 13, 27
Saliva substitutes, 63
Salivant, 63
Schizoaffective disorder, 113, 124,
    130
Schizophrenia, 19, 113, 124
    catatonic type, 130
    depression and, 130
    paranoid type, 119
Schizophreniform disorder, 115,
    124
Seasonal affective disorder (SAD),
    82–83
Seasonal depression, 82–83,
    114–15, 135–36
Sedation, **57**, 58, 64, 69
Self-help groups, 100–1
Senile dementia, 21, 129

Separation anxiety disorder, 127
Serax, 76
Serotonin, 18, 62
Sertraline, 56, **57**, 62, 66
Sex drive, 3, 97–98
Shaking, 59
Shock therapy. *See*
    Electroconvulsive therapy
Side effects of antidepressants,
    58–60, **57**, 91–93
    blurred vision, 58, 59
    constipation, 3, 58, 59, 63
    difficulty urinating, 58, 59
    dry mouth, 3, 58, 59, 62–63
    due to newer vs. older drugs,
      66
    headache, 59
    increased heart rate, 58, 59
    insomnia, 33, 59, 124–25
    late-appearing, 98–99
    memory impairment, 58, 59
    nausea, 3–4, 59
    orthostatic hypotension, 58,
      59, 63–64, 68
    restlessness, nervousness,
      agitation, 3, 33, 64, 68,
      78, 125
    severity of, 97
    sex drive, 3, 97–98
    shaking, 59
    skin rash, 59
    sleepiness, **57**, 58, 64, 69
    weight gain or loss, 33, 59,
      65–66, 68
Sinequan, **57**
Single photon emission computed
    tomography (SPECT), 37
SK-Pramine, 56, **57**
Skin rash, 59
Sleep deprivation, 83–84
Sleep disturbances
    in depression, 3–4, 22, 33,
      58–59, 124–25

    in manic episode, 116
Sleepiness, **57**, 58, 64, 69
"Smiling depression," 3–4
Sociability, 117
Speech, 116–17
Steroids, 11, 24
Stimulant drugs, 74
Stool softeners, 63
Styron, William, 9
Suicide, 15, 19, 33, 39–42, 128
    in adolescents, 19, 91
    antidepressants and, 67, 98
    in children, 91
    incidence of, 39–40
    risk factors for, 40–41
    thoughts of, 40, 126
Supportive psychotherapy, 43, 46
Surfax, 63
Surmontil, **57**
Swimming, 82

Talk therapy. *See* Psychotherapy
Tardive dyskinesia, 76
Tegretol, 75
    during pregnancy, 89
Thiothixene, 56
Thorazine, 55–56, 72
Thought disorder, 19
Thyroid disorders, 11, 24, 99
Thyroid hormone, 74
Tofranil, 56, **57**
Tranxene, 76
Tranylcypromine, 68, **68**
Trazodone, 56, **57**, 66
Treatment of depression, 43–44,
    108–9
    antidepressants, 44, 53–76
    in children, 19
    deciding when to treat, 27–28
    effectiveness of, 25–26, 44
    in elderly, 21–22
    electroconvulsive therapy
      (ECT), 44, 77–79

Treatment of depression (cont.)
  exercise, 81–82
  length of, 88–89
  for mild depression, 25
  phototherapy, 82–83
  placebo studies, 50
  psychosurgery, 84
  psychotherapy, 43, 45–52
  questions about, 85–101
  selecting best treatment, 54, 86
  sleep deprivation, 83–84
  who should treat, 85–86
Tremor, 59
Triavil, 75
Trimipramine, 57
L-Tryptophan, 74
Twins, 10
Tyramine-containing foods, 68, 70–71

"Uppers," 26, 96
Urinary difficulty, 58, 59

VA Oralube, 63
Valium, 76
Valproate, 75
  during pregnancy, 89–90
Vitamin deficiencies, 24, 92–93
Vitamin supplements, 92–93
Vivactil, 57

Wakefield Self-Report
    Questionnaire, 29–31
Walking, 82
Weight gain or loss, 3, 33, 59, 65–66, 68
Wellbutrin, 56, 57, 62, 66
Worthlessness, 33–34, 125

Xanax, 76
Xero-Lube, 63

Zoloft, 56, 57, 62, 66
Zung Self-Rating Depression
    Scale, 28